establishing
effective
discipline
for your children

homebuilders

PARENTING SERIES®

establishing
effective
discipline
for your children

by
dennis & barbara
rainey

Little Rock, Arkansas

ESTABLISHING EFFECTIVE DISCIPLINE FOR YOUR CHILDREN
FamilyLife Publishing®
5800 Ranch Drive
Little Rock, Arkansas 72223
1-800-FL-TODAY • FamilyLife.com
FLTI, d/b/a FamilyLife®, is a ministry of Campus Crusade for Christ International®

Unless otherwise noted, Scripture quotations are from the Holy Bible, English Standard Version, copyright © 2001 by Crossway Bibles, a division of Good News Publishers. Used by permission. All rights reserved.

Scripture quotations marked (NIV) are taken from the Holy Bible, New International Version®. NIV®. Copyright © 1973, 1978, 1984 by Biblica, Inc. All rights reserved worldwide. Used by permission.

ISBN: 978-1-60200-351-4

The HomeBuilders Parenting Series® is a registered trademark of FLTI, d/b/a FamilyLife.

Design: Brand Navigation, LLC

Cover image: Masterfile Corporation

Printed in the United States of America

14 13 12 11 10   1 2 3 4 5

FAMILYLIFE

Unless the LORD builds the house,
those who build it labor in vain.

PSALM 127:1

The HomeBuilders Parenting Series®

Improving Your Parenting
Establishing Effective Discipline for Your Children
Guiding Your Teenagers
Raising Children of Faith

The HomeBuilders Couples Series®

Building Your Marriage to Last
Improving Communication in Your Marriage
Resolving Conflict in Your Marriage
Mastering Money in Your Marriage
Building Teamwork in Your Marriage
Growing Together in Christ
Building Up Your Spouse
Managing Pressure in Your Marriage

welcome to homebuilders

When we bring a new life into the world, we burst with pride and joy... but are often unprepared to raise that child to become a mature, responsible adult.

In response to this need, FamilyLife has developed the HomeBuilders Parenting Series with several goals in mind: (1) to encourage you and help you not to feel overwhelmed by the responsibilities of parenting, (2) to help you develop a practical and biblical plan for parenting, (3) to enhance and strengthen your teamwork as a couple, (4) to help you connect with other parents so you can encourage and help one another, and (5) to help you strengthen your relationship with God.

You will notice as you proceed through this study that the Bible is cited as the authority on issues of life, marriage, and parenting. The Bible is God's Word—his blueprint for building a godly home and for dealing with the practical issues of living. Although written nearly two thousand years ago, Scripture still speaks clearly and powerfully about the concerns we face in our families.

A Special Word to Single Parents

Although the primary audience for this study is married couples, we recognize that single parents can also benefit from the experience. If you are a single parent, you will find that while some of the language may not be directed to your circumstances, the teaching and principles are highly applicable and can help you develop a solid, workable plan for your family.

Do we really need to be part of a group? Couldn't we just go through this study as a couple?

While you could work through the study as a couple, you would miss the opportunity to connect with friends and to learn from one another's experiences. You will find that the questions in each session not only help you grow closer to your spouse, but they also create an environment of warmth and fellowship with other couples as you study together.

What does it take to lead a HomeBuilders group?

Leading a group is much easier than you may think, because the leader is simply a facilitator who guides the participants through the discussion questions. You are not teaching the material but are helping the couples discover and apply biblical truths. The special dynamic of a HomeBuilders group is that couples teach themselves.

The study guide you're holding has all the information and guidance you need to participate in or lead a HomeBuilders group. You'll find leader's notes in the back of the guide, and additional helps are posted online at FamilyLife.com/HomeBuilders.

What is the typical schedule?

Most studies in the HomeBuilders Parenting Series are six to eight weeks long, indicated by the number of sessions in the guide. The sessions are designed to take sixty minutes in the group with a project for the couples to complete between sessions.

Isn't it risky to talk about your family in a group?

The group setting should be enjoyable and informative—and nonthreatening. **THREE SIMPLE GROUND RULES** will help ensure that everyone feels comfortable and gets the most out of the experience:

1. Share nothing that will embarrass your spouse or violate the trust of your children.
2. You may pass on any question you do not want to answer.
3. If possible, as a couple complete the HomeBuilders project between group sessions.

What other help does FamilyLife offer?

Our list of marriage and family resources continues to grow. Visit FamilyLife.com to learn more about our:

- Weekend to Remember® getaway and other events;
- slate of radio broadcasts, including the nationally syndicated *FamilyLife Today*®, *Real FamilyLife with Dennis Rainey*®, and *FamilyLife This Week*®;
- multimedia resources for small groups, churches, and community networking;
- interactive products for parents, couples, small-group leaders, and one-to-one mentors; and
- assortment of blogs, forums, and other online connections.

The house is quiet, calm, and orderly. Although your host has told you otherwise, you think to yourself, "Surely there are no children living here." But as he escorts you into the living room, you're surprised to see two toddler boys contentedly watching a video, while just a few feet away their mother sings a lullaby as she gently rocks their baby sister to sleep.

You've never seen a home so peaceful. "Is it always this way?" you ask. "Is your family always this happy and contented?"

"Oh yes," your host replies. "We're blessed. The children rarely misbehave. I guess that's because ...

We interrupt this dream to bring you back to reality.

All children misbehave. They resist you, fight with their siblings, and on some days seem determined to topple the government. "Folly," we've been told, "is bound up in the heart of a child" (Proverbs 22:15). It's in the very nature of children to need correction at times, to need their wills overcome and redirected.

We certainly don't promise a perfect home life. But the ideas presented in this study can move your family in the right direction as you learn biblical principles for correcting and training your children. It will also help you, as a couple, to work together during those early years when many couples lose touch and begin drifting apart.

—Dennis & Barbara Rainey

contents

1

Purposeful
Discipline

To develop an effective plan for disciplining your children, you must first understand that discipline is a biblically mandated responsibility.

Photo Op

Introduce yourself and share one thing you're hoping to gain by participating in this study. After everyone has been introduced, take turns telling the group about your children. If you have photos of your children with you, show them off. Tell the group

- your children's full names and why you chose those names,
- their ages, and
- their grades in school, if applicable.

blueprints

Our firstborn was sweet and compliant as a young child, and we wondered why other parents seemed to have such difficulty in the area of discipline. As she grew up, and then as we had more children, we learned why! We were shocked that these angelic little children could sometimes be so willful and disobedient. At the same time, we discovered that each of us had a different approach to discipline, and we realized we needed to come up with a biblical plan that we both agreed upon.

Parents know that discipline is a vital part of their responsibility, but they often don't think they know how to do it effectively, and they feel paralyzed.

Case Study

Evan and Laura have two young children, ages seven and two, and a third child is due in a few months. Evan works full-time, and Laura supplements their income by selling jewelry part-time. They love being parents, but they didn't anticipate how difficult it would be to discipline their children.

Their seven-year-old, Brandon, is an active boy who seems to be filled with endless energy and curiosity. He is constantly climbing, running, and touching everything. In the past few months, problems have begun surfacing. First, he won't complete simple tasks, such as putting away his toys and picking up his room. For example, Brandon is responsible for cleaning his bedroom every week, but lately he never does until Laura orders him to several times and then threatens punishment unless he complies. Second, he has begun stealing snacks and lying when he's caught. Laura recently found candy wrappers under his bed, and when she confronted Brandon about it, he blamed a neighborhood friend.

Two-year-old Leslie constantly challenges her parents with her strong will. She wants to do what she wants, and on her time schedule. Laura sometimes feels that a day with her daughter is like a day on a battlefield. When Leslie doesn't get her way, she'll cry, whine, and throw temper tantrums. Leslie doesn't act like this as much around Evan, and he tells Laura that her problem is giving in to Leslie's demands too often. Laura's reply is, "I'm the one who's with her all day. You have no idea what I'm facing here!"

Evan and Laura often feel weary and overwhelmed when it comes to training and disciplining their children. They didn't know it would be such an all-consuming, seemingly endless process. They worry about whether they are spoiling their children, but they also worry about whether spanking or other types of punishments are good for them. They wonder, *How should we discipline Brandon and Leslie, and how often? If we don't maintain control over them now, what will they be like when they're teenagers?*

1. Can you relate to the problems Evan and Laura are facing? If so, in what way?

2. What questions about disciplining your children do you wrestle with?

3. Why do you think so many parents struggle with how to effectively discipline their children?

Human Nature

Samuel Taylor Coleridge, a nineteenth-century British poet, one day was embroiled in a lively discussion with a friend about religion. His friend argued that children shouldn't be given a formal Christian education but should instead be free to choose their own beliefs when they're old enough to decide about God for themselves. Coleridge grew frustrated in the debate and invited his friend to his backyard.

"You call this a garden?" the visitor exclaimed. "There are nothing but weeds here!"

"Well, you see," Coleridge replied, "I did not wish to infringe upon the liberty of the garden in any way. I was just giving the garden a chance to express itself."

4. What do you think would happen with a child who, from birth, is left totally free to select what he or she wants to do and believe? Describe how you think this child would think and act as a young adult.

5. When the Bible speaks of the "heart," it means the core essence of a person—the place where the mind, the emotions, and the will come together. What do the following passages tell us about the condition of a person's heart? Why do you think it's important for us to remember the condition of a child's heart as we raise him or her?

- Jeremiah 17:9

- Proverbs 22:15

- Romans 3:23

The Purpose of Discipline

Surveys of Christian parents have shown that their top desire is to raise children who will grow up to walk with God. With that overall objective in mind, one of our primary responsibilities as parents is to build God-honoring character in our children. We define *character* as "response-ability"—how your child responds to authority, to others, and to life's circumstances. For example, a person we would describe as "honest" is a person who has learned how to respond with the truth no matter what the circumstances. An "obedient" person has learned how to respond correctly to authority—and to God. As parents, our assignment is to cultivate and train our children to love God. And as our children learn to love him, they'll want to obey him as well.

6. What do the following verses from Proverbs tell us about why discipline is such a critical part of character training for children?

Bible verse	Benefits of discipline
Proverbs 6:23	
Proverbs 13:18	
Proverbs 15:32	
Proverbs 19:27	
Proverbs 29:15	
Proverbs 29:17	

homebuilders principle: Discipline is an essential part of character training because it helps children understand the consequences of foolish choices.

God's Model

Throughout the Bible we find that God not only *tells* us how to respond to other people; he also *shows* us how through the example of his relationship with us. We're commanded, for example, to forgive others as Christ has forgiven us (Colossians 3:13). Husbands are also told to love their wives as Christ loved the church (Ephesians 5:25).

So it is with discipline. As Deuteronomy 8:5 tells us, "Know then in your heart that, as a man disciplines his son, the LORD your God disciplines you."

7. Read Hebrews 12:4–11. What do we learn about why God disciplines his children? In light of this passage, why should you discipline your children?

8. In what ways does God discipline us as adults, and why do we need it?

9. Hebrews 12:6 reminds us that "the Lord disciplines the one he loves." Why is it essential for you to continually follow God's model and show your unconditional love for your children? How would they feel about your efforts to discipline them if you didn't demonstrate this love?

 homebuilders principle: Just as God disciplines you out of love, you have the responsibility to discipline your children as a demonstration of your love for them.

Parting Thought

If there's one thing we've learned in the process of raising children, it's this: Nobody does it perfectly. We could fill a book just with stories of the mistakes we've made while raising six children. But in the process, we've learned the wisdom of the Bible's directions on discipline. Our goal for this study is to help you develop a practical and achievable plan for how you'll apply these biblical principles with your children. And in the process, we hope you'll strengthen your relationship with your spouse and improve your ability to work as a team in parenting.

make a date

Set a time for you and your spouse to complete the HomeBuilders project together before the next group meeting. You will be asked at the next session to share an insight or experience from the project.

date _____ time _____

location _____

homebuilders project

On Your Own

1. Before you became a parent, what was your attitude toward how children should be disciplined?

2. In what ways has your attitude or approach to discipline changed since you became a parent?

3. In what ways do you think your own upbringing has influenced your approach to discipline?

4. When it comes to the challenge of disciplining your children,

   • what do you think you're doing well?

- in what areas do you struggle?

- if you could change or improve one thing, what would it be and why?

5. In the group session, we discussed the condition of the human heart—the fact that all of us are born foolish, selfish, and sinful. What evidence have you seen in your children that foolishness and selfishness come naturally to them?

6. Complete the following sentence: "I need to discipline my children because . . ."

With Your Spouse

1. Share your responses to the questions you answered on your own. Listen carefully to your spouse's perspective, without interrupting.

2. Create a list of the things you feel you're doing well in training and disciplining your children.

3. Determine one action you can take this week to help train or discipline your children more effectively.

4. Close in prayer, asking God for wisdom as you seek to establish effective discipline for your children.

Be sure to check out the related Parent-Child Interactions beginning on page 83.

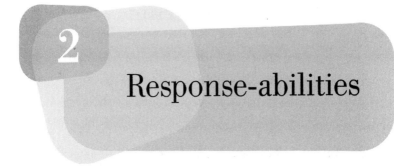

Response-abilities

Scriptural truths provide the foundation for building character in your children.

Following Instructions

Choose one or two of the following and share them with the group.

- Something one of your parents taught you to do well
- A time you were glad you followed directions
- A time you chose not to follow directions, and the outcome
- One biblical instruction you look to for guidance in life

PICTURE THIS

Do this exercise for a fun, hands-on experience. (Group Leader: See Leader's Notes for more information.)

As a group, spend five minutes trying to build or put something together that requires assembly, but do it without looking at the directions. After the time is up, discuss these questions:

- What emotions did you experience during this exercise?
- How important is it to have the right instructions? Explain.
- How is trying to build or create something without instructions like a child who doesn't receive training from his or her parents?

Project Report

If you completed the HomeBuilders project from the first session, share one thing you learned.

blueprints

Establishing a game plan for disciplining and rewarding our children is a critical part of our responsibility as parents. In this session we'll talk about the first step in establishing this plan: instruction.

As parents we understand that we have a responsibility to teach our children. Most of us, however, have given little thought to exactly what we want to impart to our children.

If we wish to be effective in parenting, we need to know not only what we want to teach our children but also how we're going to pass on these instructions.

Our Instruction Manual

1. Read 2 Timothy 3:16–17. What does this passage tell us about the Bible as the source of our instruction? Why do we need God's Word to instruct our children?

Our Responsibility

2. Read Deuteronomy 6:5–9 and Ephesians 6:4. What observations do you make from these passages about the following:

   - *what* we are to teach our children?

   - *how* we are to teach our children?

Your Children's Response-ability

As we mentioned in session 1, building character in our children is an essential component of biblical instruction—training them how to respond correctly to authority, to others, and to life's circumstances. These are critical issues of life, and they should be the focus of our instruction and of any discipline that flows from it.

Take a closer look at each of these three important areas.

Responding to Authority

The first authority in a child's life is his or her parents. Ephesians 6:1 instructs children to "obey your parents in the Lord." As you teach and train your children to obey you, they learn to trust you. They also learn that you really do love them and know what's best for them. But the learning doesn't stop there—ultimately you are shaping and training their hearts to trust God and to obey what Scripture teaches about life.

3. What can happen when a mom or dad neglects being an authority in a child's life and wants to be more of a friend than a parent?

4. Which of the following negative responses to your authority have you experienced with your children? Circle three or four that seem to be the most frequent or recurring in your home.

- acting defiantly
- being sassy
- ignoring instruction

- giving excuses
- arguing
- procrastinating
- complaining
- criticizing
- twisting your words
- expressing inappropriate anger
- having temper tantrums
- rejecting responsibility
- blaming others
- interrupting
- lying
- questioning belligerently
- cheating
- sneaking
- acting disrespectfully
- whining
- behaving rudely
- making sarcastic remarks
- other: _____

Of the responses you circled, which one bothers you the most? Why?

5. Have you ever dealt with one of the negative responses from the list and had a positive outcome? If so, share your experience with the group.

Responding to Others

Children need to learn how to relate to others in a responsible way. By design, God uses the family unit as a safe haven where parents can train children how to love and forgive, as well as how to show patience and kindness to others. For children, the early years are a crucial time for these lessons to take root.

6. Responding properly to others is a recurring theme throughout the Bible. With each couple taking one or more of the following passages, read the verses with your spouse and discuss what they teach about how we should relate to others. Then report to the group, giving a summary of your passage and your insights.

- John 13:34–35
- Romans 12:10–18
- Romans 13:8–10
- Ephesians 4:1–3
- Philippians 2:1–4
- Colossians 3:12–14

Responding to Life's Circumstances

Life is full of things we can't control—things that "just happen." We can't control traffic lights, and we can't control whether our children get sick. We can't control when we're struck by tragedy or suffering. How we respond to the circumstances of life is a major test of character.

7. What are some of life's circumstances that have been a challenge for you or your family recently? How did you respond? How did your children respond?

8. What do the following passages teach us about responding to difficult circumstances in life? If you were teaching these principles to your children, what would you say about how to apply them in their lives?

   • Matthew 6:25–34

   • Romans 8:28–32

   • James 1:2–8

homebuilders principle: By teaching children how to respond to authority, to others, and to life's circumstances, they learn that "life isn't about me, it's about God."

A United Front

It's clear that children need us to train them in response-ability. That's a big enough challenge in itself, but when two people—with different backgrounds and different approaches to discipline—are given the assignment to do this together, it becomes even more difficult.

Case Study

Melissa has strong convictions about establishing strict routines for her children and about training them to be respectful and obedient. Her husband, Ryan, respects these convictions but says he's either too tired or too stressed to help keep the children to these routines, which makes it very difficult to ever discipline them for disobedience. He usually ends up compromising, and then Melissa, wanting to avoid conflict with her husband, backs down.

Melissa says she feels she's in a no-win situation—"I either compromise my marriage or my children." She doesn't want to act domineering toward Ryan, but if she follows the pattern he sets, she fears she'd actually be teaching their children not to show respect. Not disciplining their children, to her, would be "the greatest form of child abuse."

9. What would you say to Ryan and Melissa about the steps they should take to develop a more unified approach in parenting?

homebuilders principle: You and your spouse need to work together to teach and train your children how to respond to authority, to others, and to life's circumstances.

make a date

Set a time for you and your spouse to complete the HomeBuilders project together before the next group meeting. You will be asked at the next session to share an insight or experience from the project.

date _____ time _____

location _____

On Your Own

1. Look back over the questions from the group session, and name one insight or challenge you received.

2. Look at the list "What We Want to Teach Our Children" at the end of this project (pages 25-26). Circle two or three items from this list that you would like to focus on with your children in the next few weeks.

3. As you think about each of your children, in what ways are they being tested in their responses to authority, to others, and to life's circumstances? Record your answers in the chart that follows. Be specific. Think about what you've observed recently in their behavior. (For now, leave the last question—what should we focus on in the next few weeks?—blank. You'll revisit this chart with your spouse later.)

Child _____

How is my child being tested in responding to authority?

How is my child being tested in responding to others?

How is my child being tested in responding to life's circumstances?

What should we focus on in the next few weeks?

Child _____

How is my child being tested in responding to authority?

How is my child being tested in responding to others?

How is my child being tested in responding to life's circumstances?

What should we focus on in the next few weeks?

Child _____

How is my child being tested in responding to authority?

How is my child being tested in responding to others?

How is my child being tested in responding to life's circumstances?

What should we focus on in the next few weeks?

4. Think about a specific time when you and your spouse weren't united in your approach to a discipline issue. What was the result?

Looking back, what should you have done differently?

With Your Spouse

1. Discuss your responses to the questions you answered on your own.

2. Decide on one action point you'd like to implement with each of your children to help them learn how to respond properly to authority, to others, or to life's circumstances. Record your action points on the chart on page 23.

3. Discuss what you can do to become more united in your approach to disciplining your children.

4. Close in prayer, with each of you completing this sentence: *"Dear God, my specific prayer for our children is . . ."*

Be sure to check out the related Parent-Child Interactions beginning on page 83.

WHAT WE WANT TO
TEACH OUR CHILDREN

This is part of a list we began developing years ago to capture some of the most important things we want to teach our children. Some of these lessons begin during the first year of life, while others are emphasized at later ages. Perhaps this can be the basis of a similar list for your family.

1. Above all, fear God.
2. Respect authority—trust and obey your parents.
3. Value friendships.
4. Love Christ and focus on your relationship with him, not just on doctrine or on biblical principles.
5. Show compassion for the poor.
6. Believe God for too much rather than too little.
7. Real strength is found in serving, not in being served.
8. Moral purity and a clean conscience are powerful safeguards for life.
9. Motivate people without manipulating them.
10. Learn how to handle failure with a positive, teachable attitude.
11. Keep your promises.
12. Harness the power of the tongue for good, not for evil.
13. Give too much rather than too little.
14. Always remember the importance of manners and common courtesies.
15. View life through God's eyes and follow his agenda—the Great Commission (Matthew 28:19–20) and the Greatest Commandment (Matthew 22:37).
16. Give thanks to God in all things.
17. Recognize the importance of prayer.
18. Develop the art of asking good questions and carrying on good conversations.

continued

19. Seek to grow as a Christian.
20. Learn how to handle temptation.
21. Ask God for opportunities to share with others how to know Christ.
22. Seek wisdom—skill in everyday living.
23. Gain a sense of God's direction and destiny for your life.
24. Stay teachable and don't become cynical.
25. Obtain God-honoring counsel.
26. Plans get changed, so remain flexible and adaptable.
27. Truth is best passed on through relationships.
28. Leave a legacy of holiness.
29. Keep life manageable.
30. Tame selfishness—learn you can't always get your way.
31. Choices are yours to make, and results are yours to experience.
32. Respect the dignity of another person.
33. Be faithful in the little things.
34. Character is the basis of all leadership.
35. Life isn't fair—don't compare yourself with or be jealous of others.
36. Live by commitments, not feelings.
37. Express grace and forgiveness toward others.
38. Hate the things that God hates.
39. Acknowledge the authority of Christ in your life.
40. Handle your finances wisely and responsibly.

3

Boundaries

Setting boundaries is an important element of character building for your children.

warm-up

Playground Monitor

You're conducting a study of children's play habits at two different elementary schools. Both schools have outdoor playgrounds with plenty of grass and play equipment, and bordering each school are city streets with heavy traffic. The only difference? One playground has a fence around it, and the other doesn't.

- How would you feel about sending your children to the school that isn't fenced in?
- What differences would you expect to find in the play habits of the children from these two schools?
- How would you compare a schoolyard fence to the boundaries we establish with our children?

Project Report

Share one thing you learned from the previous session's Home-Builders project.

blueprints

A Part of Life

Boundaries give order to our lives. They are the laws that govern our behavior and the expectations we set for ourselves and for others. They are the manners, biblical morality, expected behavior, and household rules that we teach our children. We may not always like the boundaries in our lives, but they are unavoidable.

1. Are you more or less strict with your children than your parents were with you? Why?

2. How do each of your children respond to the boundaries in their lives?

3. Why are boundaries necessary? As a group, list as many reasons as you can for why boundaries are good for your children.

🔲 **homebuilders principle:** Boundaries are a natural part of the teaching and training program for your children.

Biblical Boundaries

The Bible often compares God's relationship with us to our relationship with our children. So it is with the subject of setting boundaries. In Genesis 2:16–17, God tells Adam, "You may surely eat of every tree of the garden, but of the tree of the knowledge of good and evil you shall not eat, for in the day that you eat of it you shall surely die."

Throughout the Bible we're called to obey God and follow the boundaries he has set for our lives. We're also exhorted to teach his commands to our children.

4. Read Deuteronomy 6:17–25. What benefits to obeying God's commands—observing the boundaries he sets for our lives—do you find here?

5. When we talk about God's laws or boundaries, many
   people naturally think of the Ten Commandments. Look
   up this list of commandments in Exodus 20:1–17. With
   your spouse, select one commandment, answer the following questions, and then share your insights with the group.

   • What are the benefits you gain by obeying this
     commandment?

   • If you were teaching your children how to apply this
     commandment in their lives, what would you say?
     Be specific.

homebuilders principle: God sets an example for parenting
by giving you boundaries that provide direction and security
and that ultimately point you to your need to trust him with
your life.

Setting Boundaries for Your Children

6. Give one or two examples of boundaries you set for your children in the following areas:

   - household rules

   - biblical morality

   - manners

   - relating to others

7. What do your children tend to do when a particular boundary hasn't been defined very clearly? Give a specific example.

8. What do you think often happens when parents

- set too few boundaries for their children?

- set too many boundaries?

- change boundaries without telling their children?

9. Read Ephesians 6:4. How might boundaries potentially exasperate our children? Give an example of a boundary you've faced (one set by a parent, teacher, coach, or employer) that had an adverse effect on you.

make a date

Set a time for you and your spouse to complete the HomeBuilders project together before the next group meeting. You will be asked at the next session to share an insight or experience from the project.

date _____ time _____

location _____

Looking Ahead

We encourage you to make it a priority to complete the Home-Builders projects. The next few projects give you the opportunity to develop a written list of boundaries and determine appropriate consequences for your children's choices.

homebuilders project

On Your Own

1. Looking back at your childhood, identify a boundary your mom or dad set that you

   - felt was too strict or too loose.

   - intentionally crossed and then experienced a consequence. (What was the consequence?)

   - didn't care for at the time but are now glad was in place.

2. What did this session reveal to you—good or bad—about the boundaries you have for your children?

3. Use the following questions to help you evaluate the boundaries you currently have for your children:

- What do you think about the number of boundaries you have set—too many, too few, or just about right?

- Would you say that your children know the boundaries you have set? If not, why do you think they don't?

- Have you set boundaries for your children that are too general or vague? If yes, what are they?

- Are any of your boundaries unrealistic or too difficult for your children? If yes, which ones?

- What standard do you use to determine appropriate boundaries?

- How well do you enforce the boundaries you set? Are you too strict? too lenient? Explain your answer.

4. What character issues are you facing right now with your children that require clear boundaries? (You may want to refer back to the chart you completed on page 23 in the previous session's HomeBuilders project.)

With Your Spouse

1. Discuss your responses to the questions you answered on your own.

2. Discuss existing boundaries you've set with your children that need to be changed, clarified, or dropped. Write these down, as you may want to refer to them in a future Home-Builders project.

3. Talk about specific areas where you haven't set boundaries but feel they're needed.

4. End this session with prayer, asking God for wisdom, discernment, and courage as you set and enforce boundaries with your children.

Be sure to check out the related Parent-Child Interactions beginning on page 83.

4

Consequences, Part 1

Your children need to experience the consequences of both their good and poor choices.

warm-up

Take Your Pick

With your spouse, choose one of the following scenarios to review. (Pick the one that most closely corresponds to the age of your oldest child living at home.) Read the scenario and answer the discussion questions at the end. Then share your answers and insights with the group.

Scenario 1—Preschool Child

You've just moved into a new home with a big front yard where the neighborhood children love to play. Your four-year-old son, Justin, seems to be a natural organizer, but he's also selfish and bossy. When he sets up a game, he wants to be in charge and tell people what they can and can't do. When they all play with toys, you notice that he consistently takes toys away from other children and forces them to play with something else.

Scenario 2—Elementary-School-Age Child

You're training your three children to do various chores around the house. Each has a different responsibility each week. Your middle child, eight-year-old Melanie, often does her chores half-heartedly. When she sweeps the kitchen floor, she misses part of it. When she scrubs the bathtub, she lazily wipes off the loose dirt but never tries to scrub off stains. When you mention that she's not cleaning as she should, she says you're too picky.

Scenario 3—Teenager

When your daughter Bethany turned sixteen, you began allowing her to drive one of the family cars. Since then, you've noticed a streak of independence that she hadn't displayed before. You don't mind her using the car, but you do mind her attitude. She feels it's her right to have total access to the car, even when you need it. She also doesn't want to tell you where she's going or whom she's meeting. When you vaguely mention setting some rules about her social life, she declares that all of her friends have their own cars, and their parents let them do whatever they please.

1. Based on what we've learned in this study up to this point, what opportunity do you see to build character into the life of this child?

2. What boundaries do you feel are appropriate for this scenario?

Project Report

Share one thing you learned from the previous session's Home-Builders project.

Sowing and Reaping

There is a design and rhythm to life that can be summed up in the words of Galatians 6:7: "Whatever one sows, that will he also reap." We call this the "Law of Sowing and Reaping"—the fact that there are consequences to the choices we make in life. We receive benefits for staying within the boundaries, and we reap negative consequences when we don't.

This pattern was established by God in the garden of Eden. Adam and Eve experienced the joy of intimate fellowship with God until they disobeyed and ate from the Tree of the Knowledge of Good and Evil. As described in Genesis 3, God responded to their disobedience with swift discipline: First, they experienced the emotional pain of being banished from the garden—the intimate relationship they had enjoyed with the Lord changed. God also disciplined them by multiplying the pain of childbirth and cursing the ground, forcing Adam to toil for their sustenance (Genesis 3:16–19). But these aren't the only consequences we can observe in how God deals with us.

1. Give an example of a choice you made in your life (as a student, in your marriage or family, or at work) that led to immediate and direct consequences—either good or bad.

2. Read Deuteronomy 30:15–20, in which God describes to the Israelites the consequences of their choices to obey and walk with him or to disobey and turn away from him. How are these consequences like those we face for the choices we make?

3. Why do you think it's important for parents to take responsibility to communicate to their children the consequences
they will face for their actions or inaction?

Types of Consequences

To better enforce the boundaries you set for your children, it's
important to think through the types of consequences, both positive and negative, that will help build their character. Although
consequences can take a number of forms, let's look at the following areas:

- praise and rewards
- reproof and punishment
- natural consequences

Praise and Rewards

When determining a discipline plan for their children, many parents overlook the need to reinforce right choices.

4. Why is it important to consistently praise and encourage
your children when they make good choices?

5. Describe an occasion—either as a child or an adult—when a parent or authority figure in your life said something positive to you for doing something right. Why do you think you remember this experience?

---

homebuilders principle: Your children need to hear praise and affirmation for the good choices they make.

Reproof and Punishment

We define *reproof* and *punishment* as a "measured amount of pain, administered by a loving parent, appropriate to the offense." Depending on the offense, this "pain" may be a spanking, or it may be a time-out or the removal of a privilege. In many cases, this pain may be the only thing that can impart to a child the wisdom of living within boundaries.

Some parents use corporal punishment (spanking) as their only form of discipline. We'll focus more on spanking in the next session, but it's important to realize that reproof can take many other forms, depending on the type of offense and the age of the child.

6. Read Proverbs 19:18 and Ecclesiastes 8:11. What is the danger of not using any type of reproof or punishment with children?

7. What are some punishments—other than spanking—that can be used to help children of the following age groups experience consequences for their poor choices?

- two to three years of age

- four to eight years of age

- nine to twelve years of age

- thirteen to eighteen years of age

homebuilders principle: To curb sinful behavior, children need to experience punishment—a measured amount of pain—in a timely manner for their poor choices.

Natural Consequences

There will be times when you won't need to punish a child yourself for poor choices. Sometimes children learn their most significant lessons when they are allowed to experience the natural consequences of their poor choices.

8. Look at the following list. What can happen when a child does these things? What are some of the natural consequences you could let a child experience related to each of these behaviors?

- Staying up too late

- Procrastinating on a homework assignment

- Eating too much junk food

- Not going to the bathroom when Mommy or Daddy says to

- Oversleeping

- Not locking a school locker or bike

- Cheating on a test

9. Describe a time when you let your children experience natural consequences. Was it difficult to watch this happen and not intervene? Explain.

make a date

Set a time for you and your spouse to complete the HomeBuilders project together before the next group meeting. You will be asked at the next session to share an insight or experience from the project.

date _____ time _____

location _____

homebuilders project

On Your Own

1. What key point from this session is most relevant to your family right now?

2. The first part of the group discussion focused on the consequences God brings into our lives when we obey or disobey him. As you look back over your life, when did you experience

   • God's blessings for a right choice?

   • God's discipline?

3. How would you rate yourself at praising and rewarding your children for their good choices? Explain your answer.

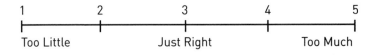

4. How would you rate yourself at disciplining your children (with reproof and punishment) for their poor choices? Explain your answer.

5. How would you rate yourself at allowing your children to experience the natural consequences of their actions? Explain your answer.

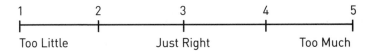

6. Which area do you feel is your weakest? What one step could you take to improve in this area?

---

7. For the following statements, indicate your level of agreement or disagreement.

I feel my spouse backs me up and doesn't undermine me when I discipline the children.

1	2	3	4
Strongly Agree	Somewhat Agree	Somewhat Disagree	Strongly Disagree

I back up my spouse and don't undermine him/her when he/she disciplines our children.

1	2	3	4
Strongly Agree	Somewhat Agree	Somewhat Disagree	Strongly Disagree

As a couple, we're in general agreement on matters that require discipline.

1	2	3	4
Strongly Agree	Somewhat Agree	Somewhat Disagree	Strongly Disagree

8. Name a quality you respect or admire in your spouse about the way he or she disciplines your children.

With Your Spouse

1. Discuss your responses to the questions you answered on your own.

2. Review the "Ideas for Praise and Reward" from the "Ideas List" at the end of the project. Select ideas you want to begin using with your children. Agree on a list of rewards that you would like to use to help build character in your children.

3. Review the "Ideas for Reproof and Punishment" from the "Ideas List." Select ideas you want to begin using with your children. Agree on a list of punishments that you would like to use to help build character in your children.

4. Close your time by praying for one another and for each of your children. Pray for wisdom about how to best utilize and balance praise and reward, reproof and punishment.

Be sure to check out the related Parent-Child Interactions beginning on page 83.

IDEAS LIST

Ideas for Praise and Reward

- Offer a word of praise and affirmation for good choices.
- Show physical affection: hugs and kisses.
- Give notes and cards: remember the power of the written word; encouraging notes are often read and reread.
- Engage in fun activities.
- Take your child out to dinner at a favorite restaurant.
- Go on a special date with your child.
- Throw a special celebration.
- Let your child earn points or tickets for good choices and attitudes, and then redeem them periodically for rewards with predetermined values—special desserts, toys, movie tickets, trips to a museum, family video rentals, and so on.
- Keep a chart in a public place (such as on the refrigerator), and put stars on it for good behavior and completed chores.
- Give increased privileges (later curfew, later bedtime) for showing responsibility.
- Put a designated number of beans (perhaps ten to twenty) in a small jar, and place an empty identical jar next to it. When your child does something well, move a few beans from the full jar over to the empty one. When all the beans are moved over to the other jar, treat your child to a special activity, such as going out for ice cream or a movie.

Ideas for Reproof and Punishment

- Send your child to his or her room.
- Deprive your child of something desired—dessert, television, allowance, time on the computer, a planned activity, and so on.
- Assign extra chores. Create a "Chore Box" by writing different types of chores on sheets of paper and putting them in a box. When a child misbehaves, pull a chore out of the box for him or her to perform.

- Assign special work requiring a big sacrifice of time and effort. For example, cleaning the garage, pulling weeds out of an entire flower bed, or scraping the paint off a piece of furniture you want to refinish.
- "Ground" your child by making him or her stay at home during afternoons, evenings, or weekends for a specified period of time.
- Have your child make restitution for something stolen or intentionally broken.
- Take away privileges previously earned, such as staying up later or going to a friend's house, or (for older children) driving the car or having a later curfew.

Combination Reward and Punishment Strategy

- A money jar can work well when your children are constantly arguing and fighting with each other. Begin with a specified amount of money, and then remove money for bad behavior or disobedience. At the end of the week or month, the kids keep what's left. For example, if two children are constantly arguing, put ten one-dollar bills in a jar and say, "Every time one of you makes a negative comment to the other, I'm taking out a dollar. After a week, you can split what's left. If you run out of dollars before then, I'll start reducing your allowance." The immediate consequences to your children's actions, as well as the motivation of a short-term reward, can show children that this type of behavior really is the result of the choices they make.

Note: It might be helpful to photocopy these lists and post them in a handy place. We often refer to similar lists to give us ideas when we need them.

5

Consequences, Part 2
Spanking

The Bible is not silent on the controversial subject of corporal punishment.

Note: Throughout this session the terms *corporal punishment* and *spanking* are used interchangeably.

Discipline Options

Review the following list, checking the types of discipline that were regularly used by your parents.

__ time-out   __ grounding

__ loss of privileges   __ allowance deductions

__ spanking   __ additional chores

__ lectures   __ other: _____

- For those that were used on you, in what order would you rank these types of discipline for their overall effectiveness?
- Which of these worked best on you when you were five? ten? sixteen?

Project Report

Share one thing you learned from the previous session's Home-Builders project.

Spare the Rod?

Corporal punishment is one of the most difficult and emotional topics for many parents to discuss. We often hear sharply different opinions about spanking:

> Corporal punishment in the hands of a loving parent is . . . a teaching tool by which harmful behavior is inhibited. (Dr. James Dobson, *The Strong-Willed Child*)
>
> Hitting children teaches them that it is acceptable to hit others who are smaller and weaker. (Center for Effective Discipline, "Spanking: Facts and Fiction" by Nadine Block, accessed May 10, 2010)

Spanking can be a positive force in teaching self-discipline and obedience. (Susan Alexander Yates, *And Then I Had Kids*)

Perhaps behind much of today's violence lies a simple reason almost too obvious for us to see, namely, spanking . . . Are we not in effect training inadvertently and encouraging ever so innocently more abuse and violence by continuing the malevolent practice of spanking? (Robert R. Gillogly, "Spanking Hurts Everybody," *Theology Today* 37, no. 4: 422, 424)

The rod of discipline, while it brings pain, also brings a harvest of righteousness and peace. The child whose parents use the rod in a timely, appropriate fashion learns to submit to authority. (Tedd Tripp, *Shepherding a Child's Heart*)

1. Which of the previous quotes most closely describes the attitude you've had toward spanking? Explain your answer.

2. Why do you think there is such disagreement about spanking children?

3. What are some of the cultural messages you've heard about spanking?

Searching the Scriptures

Because of abuses, corporal punishment as a method of discipline has increasingly come under fire. It is imperative that we as parents know what we believe about this subject and apply it with love and sensitivity.

4. According to the following scriptures, what are some of the benefits of corporal punishment?

- Proverbs 13:24

- Proverbs 22:15

- Proverbs 23:13–14

- Proverbs 29:15

- Hebrews 12:11

5. What do you think is unique about spanking as a form of discipline that can help bring about such profound character growth in a child?

Developing a Healthy Approach to Spanking

Many parents feel "stuck" when they consider the subject of spanking. They acknowledge what the Bible says, but it's difficult to actually do it. They feel constrained by the voices from our culture, by negative childhood experiences, or by the personal distress they feel when they have to punish their children. Following are two steps that can help.

Step 1: Develop an Overall Discipline Plan

First, you need to work together to develop an overall plan for when you will use spanking as you discipline your children. As we've discussed, there are punishments other than spanking that can work well for different offenses and in different age groups.

In developing our discipline plan, we determined to "let the punishment fit the crime." For some offenses, it worked well to use a time-out, a chore, or the loss of a privilege as punishment. Spanking was reserved for more serious offenses that revolved around critical character issues. For this we took our cue from Proverbs 6:16–19, which lists seven offenses that are detestable to the Lord. We figured if God hates these attitudes and behaviors, we ought to be diligent to focus on them with our children and treat them more seriously than minor offenses.

6. With each couple selecting at least one of the items from the following chart, talk about how this behavior is exhibited in children, and then record your answers in the right-hand column. (Some of these phrases aren't how we normally describe children, so think creatively.) Share your insights with the group.

Seven things the Lord detests (Proverbs 6:16–19)	Ways children exhibit these behaviors
"Haughty eyes" (verse 17)	
"A lying tongue" (verse 17)	
"Hands that shed innocent blood" (verse 17)	
"A heart that devises wicked plans" (verse 18)	
"Feet that make haste to run to evil" (verse 18)	
"A false witness who breathes out lies" (verse 19)	
"One who sows discord among brothers" (verse 19)	

Step 2: Administer Corporal Punishment Carefully and Lovingly

7. What are some mistakes parents make in how they spank their children?

8. Review the "Guidelines for Spanking" that follow. How does this process compare to the approach you use?

Answer questions 8 and 9 with your spouse. After answering, you may want to share an appropriate insight or discovery with the group.

9. What do you think could be improved in the way you administer corporal punishment?

GUIDELINES FOR SPANKING

As we raised six children through the various stages of development, it became apparent that each child had different needs when it came to discipline. But all of them, at times, needed a spanking. Spanking was usually not our first choice of discipline—it was a tool we used for certain acts and patterns of disobedience, and we made sure we administered it carefully and lovingly. Time after time, we remarked to each other how a child's attitude would improve when we used this particular form of discipline, and we'd wished we'd used it earlier.

We don't believe that parents should ignore a biblical concept just because some people don't apply it well. However, we do recommend that parents agree on some guidelines. When we spanked our children, we followed a simple but effective procedure:

- Do it promptly, but do it in private, not in public. (The younger the child, the greater the need for immediate discipline.)
- Make sure you're in control of yourself. Discipline should never be administered in anger.
- Take or send your child to another room.
- Look your child in the eyes and explain why he or she is being punished.
- Assure your child of your love.
- Hold your child as you spank him or her. Inflict a measure of pain, but be careful not to be too strong. (We suggest one swat for each year. For example, a three-year-old would receive three swats.)
- Use an object that will not harm your child.
- Comfort your child until he or she has finished crying.
- Look your child in the eye and talk over why he or she received a spanking, and again assure your child of your love. Ask your child to admit the offense and challenge him or her to be obedient.
- Pray with your child.

homebuilders principle: When administered properly, corporal punishment is a valuable tool for building your child's character.

make a date

Set a time for you and your spouse to complete the HomeBuilders project together before the next group meeting. You will be asked at the next session to share an insight or experience from the project.

date _____ time _____

location _____

homebuilders project

As you get together for this project, we encourage you to make it your goal to come away with a plan for corporal punishment that you both agree with. Over the years we've found that we've had to dialogue frequently to better understand each other's perspective. On a number of occasions, I (Dennis) have felt that a child was taking advantage of Barbara and that she needed me to step in to bring clarity on a plan of action. At other times, it was Barbara who was closest to the situation with a child, and she brought the clarity that was needed. In all of our discussions, we always tried to work together in coming up with a plan to deal with the issues we were facing with each of our children.

On Your Own

1. Think back to your childhood and recall a time when

   - you were punished that really stands out in your mind. What made this event memorable? How did you benefit from this experience?

- you felt you were punished unfairly. Why did you feel it was unfair?

- you should have been disciplined but weren't. What form of punishment do you think you needed at the time? Why?

2. What insight or concept from the group session do you most need to apply?

3. Up to this point, what has been your attitude about corporal punishment? In addition to your childhood experiences,

what influences would you say have most shaped your attitude about spanking?

4. How do you think your views on spanking compare to those of your spouse? How are they alike? different?

5. Check at least one area in which you could improve how you reward and discipline your children. Also check one area where you feel your spouse could improve (mark this with the letter S).

__ Be more consistent in the standards I set.

__ Be more consistent in enforcing boundaries.

__ Raise my voice less.

__ Be more involved in the discipline of our children.

__ Be more loving when I discipline.

__ Support my spouse better when he or she disciplines our children.

__ Reward our children more often.

__ Be less reactive and more in control when I discipline our children.

__ Other: _____

6. In the following chart, make a list of punishments you
   think are appropriate for different offenses.

	Offense	Punishment
Young children (age ten or under)		
Older children		

7. What one aspect of corporal punishment (perhaps a question about establishing boundaries, appropriate punishments, or a point of clarification) do you want to be sure to discuss with your spouse?

8. What boundaries have your children repeatedly been disregarding lately? What type of reproof would work best to discourage this behavior in the future?

With Your Spouse

1. Discuss your responses to the questions you answered on your own.

2. Write down two or three aspects of handling discipline and rewards that you both would like to change or improve.

3. Agree on a list of offenses that should automatically earn a spanking or an agreed-upon corresponding level of punishment.

4. Pray together, asking for God's wisdom, strength, and love as you determine and enforce your boundaries.

Be sure to check out the related Parent-Child Interactions beginning on page 83.

6

Building Your
Endurance

In running the parenting race, remember that establishing effective discipline is a marathon, not a sprint.

Case Study

For the most part, Rob and Jenna knew what they were getting into when they started a family. They knew the challenges their own parents had faced, and they felt they had developed a good biblical plan for raising their three children. They worked hard at all the different aspects of building character in their children—helping them establish a relationship with Christ, training them how to relate to other people, teaching them to work hard at their household chores, and much more.

There's only one thing they didn't expect—that they would grow so weary of teaching the same things and disciplining for the same issues over and over and over again!

"I feel like this never ends," Jenna said late one night as she fell into bed. "It seems like I never get a break. And just when I think the kids are making progress, new issues come up. I don't think these kids are ever going to change."

Each of their children was a challenge in some way: Nine-year-old Matt, for example, never seemed to be able to control his tongue. He talked back to his parents and continually ridiculed his younger brother and sister. Deena, at age seven, knew she was required to make her bed daily and clean her room three times a week, but she never did these tasks on her own. On top of that, she continually left her toys strewn around the house. And their youngest child, three-year-old Alex, was in a stage where he yelled and screamed and hit his siblings and friends when he didn't get what he wanted.

Jenna and Rob did everything they could to train their children, and they felt they used both punishments and rewards effectively. But they wondered if their children would ever learn. They wondered if Deena would still be messy when she became an adult and whether Matt would still be cutting down his family and friends when he graduated from high school. And they wondered if those problems would seem minor compared to the challenges of parenting teenagers.

It just never seemed to end. And sometimes they wondered if it was worth the effort.

- In what ways can you relate to Rob and Jenna's feelings?
- What other challenges are you facing in maintaining a plan to train and discipline your children?

Project Report

Share one thing you learned from the previous session's Home-Builders project.

Running the Parenting Race

1. Read Hebrews 12:1–3. How would you compare parenting—and especially disciplining your children—to the act of running a long-distance race?

When I (Dennis) turned forty, I began running for exercise—about 3 miles, two to three times per week. Over the years friends have encouraged me to run a marathon (26.2 miles), but I've never done it. I've never had the time to train adequately for such a monumental effort.

I have read enough about marathons to know that most runners "hit a wall" at around the 20-mile mark. They're dehydrated and light-headed, and their legs feel like mush. Only their conditioning and willpower enable them to continue.

Parenting is a marathon, not a sprint. One aspect of parenting we underestimated was the perseverance that would be demanded of us as we trained our children. We started with our daughter Ashley in August 1974, and it wasn't until the same month twenty-nine years later that we sent our sixth child to college. It's common for parents to "hit a wall" when they feel like giving up. They become weary of teaching the same things over and over and continually disciplining for the same issues. But take heart—there is hope! From Hebrews 12:1–3, let's take a closer look at three keys for maintaining the endurance needed for parenting.

Key 1: Lay Aside Whatever Hinders and Entangles You

2. During this study we've discussed a biblical plan for disciplining and rewarding children. What can hinder us from actually implementing this plan and from disciplining our children consistently?

3. Recall a time when you should have disciplined one of your children but didn't. What was the result?

Key 2: Remember That Parenting Is a Race God Has Set for You

Hebrews 12:1 exhorts us to "run with endurance the race that is set before us." Just as a marathon runner follows an established course, so we as parents follow a direction and pursue a goal set by our Lord.

4. Based on everything we've discussed in this study, what would you say is your overall goal in parenting?

5. In what way is disciplining and rewarding your children a vital part of reaching that goal?

Key 3: Keep Your Eyes on Christ

6. Read Hebrews 12:2–3 again. How can fixing your eyes on Christ help you to "not grow weary or fainthearted"? What kept Christ running his race?

7. What encouragement do each of the following scriptures offer when you feel worn out from your responsibilities as a parent?

- Joshua 1:7–9

- 1 Corinthians 15:58

- Galatians 6:9

8. Have you ever felt helpless or ineffective as a parent? Describe what happened.

9. Has there ever been a time when, as a parent, you felt especially helped by God—that he gave you extra strength or wisdom, for example, or directly answered prayer? Describe what happened.

homebuilders principle: God will give you wisdom and strength to run the race he has set for you as a parent—he loves to help the helpless!

Retrospection

As you come to the end of this study, take a few minutes to reflect on the experience. Review the following questions and write down responses to the questions you can answer. Then share with the group one or more of your answers.

- What has this group meant to you over the course of this study? Be specific.

- What is the most valuable lesson you've learned or discovered?

- How have you as a parent been changed or challenged through this study?

- What would you like to see happen next for this group?

Parting Thought

When we began our family, we had no idea that parenting would be such a marathon. Little did we know that twenty-nine years would pass before our youngest child graduated from high school. Our race has often been difficult and wearisome, and yet it has also been a greater joy and privilege than we ever could have imagined. We can echo the words of 3 John 4, which tells us, "I have no greater joy than to hear that my children are walking in the truth."

If you're unsure whether you have a personal relationship with Jesus or are frustrated with your spiritual life, be sure to read the article "Our Problems, God's Answers" in the back of this book. It will give you insight into how to become a Christian, as well as how to walk with Christ on a daily basis.

Our world needs parents like you. Our culture needs young people of character who grow up to walk closely with God and then lead others to do the same. The inspired Word of God as expressed in Hebrews 12 is worth paraphrasing and repeating: Fix your eyes on Christ and run the race God has set before you. It's worth it!

make a date

Set a time for you and your spouse to complete the HomeBuilders project together.

date _____ time _____

location _____

homebuilders project

In this project you'll "put it all together," reflecting on the themes we've discussed during this study and thinking through how they apply to each of your children. To help you, we've included an article at the end of this book, "Disciplining Your Children as They Grow" (page 137), that has age-appropriate information for building character in your children.

On Your Own

1. What point from this session had the most impact on you and why?

2. Overall, what has been the most important insight or lesson for you from this course?

3. Name one decision—something you want to do, stop doing, or change—that you reached during this study and that you need to follow through on. What needs to happen for this to become a reality?

4. Read through the sections of the "Disciplining Your Children as They Grow" article (on page 137) that pertain to the ages of each of your children. If you have a child who is close to entering another age level, read through that section as well.

5. Turn back to page 23 and look at the chart where you rated each child on how he or she responds to authority, to others, and to life's circumstances. What do you think are your child's greatest character strengths and needs?

6. What do you think are the greatest influences on each of your children right now? (For example: What are they being exposed to through the media? What is a cause of temptation for them? What type of influence are their friends having on them?) What types of influences do you anticipate they will encounter in the next two to three years?

7. What would you say are the primary boundaries you have identified as important for your children to know, and for you to enforce? And what have you determined are the appropriate consequences (both good and bad) for how these boundaries are observed by your children?

With Your Spouse

1. Congratulations—you've made it to the last project of this study! Start your time together by reflecting on what impact this course has had on you by discussing these questions:

   - What has been the best part of this study for you?
   - How has this study benefited your marriage?
   - In what ways has this course helped you as a parent?
   - What is something new you've learned or discovered about your spouse? yourself? your children?

2. Share your responses to the questions you answered on your own.

3. The chart that follows is designed to incorporate all the themes we've discussed in this study: character needs, boundaries, and consequences. Fill in a chart for each of your children. (You have permission to photocopy the chart as needed, or you may want to re-create it yourself on a separate sheet of paper.)

Child: _____

Character strengths

Character needs

Greatest present influences

Anticipated near-future influences

Needed boundaries

Consequences for overstepping boundaries

4. Evaluate what you can or should do, or continue doing, to strengthen your home. You may want to consider continuing the practice of setting aside time for date nights. You may also want to review the list of ideas in "Where Do You Go from Here?" on page 93.

5. Spend a few minutes together in prayer. Thank God for each other and for your children. Pray for God's wisdom, direction, and blessing as you continue seeking to establish effective discipline for your children.

Be sure to check out the related Parent-Child Interactions beginning on page 83.

parent-child interactions

The following six Parent-Child Interactions draw upon the numerous biblical references to plants, trees, gardens, crops, and harvests. God used these images (which were quite vivid and understandable for those living in a mostly agrarian culture) to teach enduring truths about spiritual growth.

Interaction 1

Water

For this project you'll need a small plot of soil—preferably outdoors, but an indoor pot will do—and something to plant in it, such as a flower or shrub. As an ongoing object lesson, you can tend to this plant with your children over the course of all the interactions.

1. With your children, prepare the soil and plant your flower or shrub.
2. Say: Over the next few weeks, we're going to talk about some of the things this plant needs to be healthy, and we'll also look at how the Bible compares the growth of plants, trees, and crops to how we grow in our relationship with God.
3. Have your children read Psalm 1:1–3 and Jeremiah 17:5–8. Ask:

- What do both of these passages talk about?
- Why is it important for a tree, or any other plant, to get water?
- What happens to a tree or plant that doesn't get enough water?

4. Look at Psalm 1:1–3 again, and then have your children complete the following sentence: I will be like a tree planted by a stream of water if I . . .

5. Jeremiah 17:7 says, "Blessed is the man who trusts in the LORD, whose trust is the LORD." Ask:

- What does this verse mean to you?
- Why can we trust God?

6. Psalm 1 tells us that the person whose delight is in God's law will be blessed. Ask: What do you think it means to delight in God's Word?

7. Close in prayer. Thank God for his Word, and pray that you will delight in it. Pray that your trust in God will grow stronger with each passing day.

Interaction 2

Good Soil

In this project you'll compare different types of soil and read through Christ's parable of the sower. You'll need to find a place in your yard, or perhaps in a park, where you can show your children the three bad types of soil mentioned in the parable—soil on a path, soil with rocks, and soil with weeds or thorns—so that the lesson can be seen more clearly.

1. Read Mark 4:1–8. Ask: What happens to the seeds that fall on the different types of soil?

   - pathway
   - rocky soil
   - soil with thorns
   - good soil

2. Take your children out to show them the different types of bad soil that they just read about in the passage. Begin with the pathway. Read aloud from Mark 4:13–15, and then ask: What does it mean that "Satan immediately comes and takes away the word" from the people who are like soil on the path?

3. Find some rocky soil (perhaps by the path) with some plants that have shallow roots. If possible, show how easily you can pull them out; then read Mark 4:16–17. Talk about the need for us to have deeper roots in our relationship with God so that we'll be able to withstand the problems we face in life.

4. Now find some soil with weeds or thorns; then read Mark 4:18–19. Ask: What do you think this passage means when it says that the "cares of the world" and the "desires for other things" choke out the effect of God's Word in our lives? Can you give some examples?

5. Now take your children to the plot of soil you're cultivating. Ask:

- What makes this soil good compared to the other types we've examined?
- What happens when the seed of God's Word is put in good soil? What effect does it have in our lives?

6. Close in prayer, asking God to work in your lives so that the soil of your hearts and minds will be good and ready to receive his Word.

Interaction 3

Protecting the Garden

1. Take your children to a yard, garden, or field that hasn't been cared for in some time, such as a vacant property or the banks of a ditch.
2. Ask:

- What has happened to this yard because no one has cared for it?
- Who do you think planted the weeds?

3. Have them count the different types of weeds they can find. Say: There are several places in the Bible where we can read about weeds. Have your children read Proverbs 24:30–31. Ask:

- What does this passage say about the man who had the vineyard?
- What should he have done to protect his vineyard better?
- What can we learn from this passage that applies to our lives?
- What are some examples of the boundaries—or rules—that we have set up to protect you?
- What do you think would happen if we didn't set any of these boundaries for you?

4. Close in prayer, thanking God for the boundaries he sets in your lives. Pray that the weeds of the world that would choke out God's Word would be kept back in your lives.

Interaction 4

Cutting and Pruning

In this lesson you'll discuss the process of pruning a tree or shrub and compare it to the need for parents to discipline their children. You'll need to find a plant or shrub with some unhealthy leaves or branches that can be cut off or pruned. Use your new plant or shrub if it has grown enough so that you can prune it. (Or you could visit a nursery and ask a gardener there to explain to your children why pruning is necessary for healthy growth; if you do this, begin with question 2 in the following exercise.)

1. Show your children the plant with unhealthy leaves and branches. Say: One thing that's necessary for growing

healthy plants is pruning. Branches and leaves that are dead or unhealthy are cut off. Then healthy branches are cut back to keep the branches strong and stimulate new growth. Fruit and blossoms sprout from the new growth a tree or shrub puts out every year, so pruning helps produce more.

2. Ask: What do you think would happen to a tree or plant that was never pruned?

3. Read John 15:1–5. Ask:

- In this passage who is the true vine?
- Who are the branches?
- Who is the gardener who does the pruning?
- What do you think this passage means when it says that God prunes the branches?
- What do you think God wants to cut away in our lives?

4. Now have your children read Hebrews 12:10–11. Ask: What does this passage say about why it's good for us to be disciplined by our parents? by God?

5. Say: In many ways, disciplining a child is like pruning. As parents, part of our job is to teach you how to make right choices and avoid making bad ones. Then ask: What are some of the things we've been pruning out of your lives lately? What are some of the attitudes and behaviors we've talked to you about?

6. Talk about some of the character issues you've been addressing with your children. Talk about why it's important for them to experience the consequences of their

decisions. Tell them that you're pruning them now so they'll be more responsive to God as they grow up.

7. Close in prayer, asking God to give you wisdom about the things in your lives that need to be cut and pruned for you to grow closer to God.

Interaction 5

Staying Connected to the Vine

1. Take your children out to a garden, orchard, vineyard, or nursery. Look closely at the plants and point out the fact that plants and trees have some type of main stem, trunk, or vine, as well as a number of branches that are attached to this stem or trunk. Hold one of the branches and ask:

   - What would happen to this branch if I broke it off? What would it look like tomorrow? (If it's your plant, go ahead and cut off one of the branches; then leave it there for you and your children to examine the next day.)
   - Why does a branch wither and die when it's cut off from the plant?

   After your children answer, explain that the nutrients a branch needs are contained in the main part of the plant or tree. When a branch is cut off, it no longer can get the nutrients it needs to survive.

2. Say: Last time we read a Bible passage from John that talked about vines and pruning. It said that Christ is the Vine, and we are the branches. We're going to look at these verses again, plus some others. Read John 15:1–8. Ask:

- What does Jesus say about what a branch is supposed to do?
- What do you think it means to be connected to Jesus like that? What can we do to be connected to Christ so that we'll bear fruit?

3. Read 1 John 3:24 and 1 John 4:15. Ask: What do these verses tell us about remaining connected to Christ?

4. Talk to your children about the importance of spending time with God—reading and meditating on his Word, praying, and worshipping. Mention that in the next interaction you'll talk about what happens when you remain connected to Christ: you bear fruit.

5. Close your time in prayer, asking God to keep each of you connected to Christ, just as a branch remains connected to the vine.

Interaction 6

Bearing Fruit

1. Find a fruit or nut tree to examine. (If you don't have one, contact a nursery or orchard and arrange for a visit.) Ask your children: What kind of fruit grows on

an apple tree? What kind of nuts grow on a pecan tree? (Your children may wonder why you're asking such obvious questions!)

2. Say: The point is that God made different types of trees, and the function of each type is to produce a certain kind of fruit. Read Matthew 7:16–20; then ask: In this passage, we're compared to trees. If we're good trees, we'll bear good fruit. What type of "good fruit" do you think God created us to bear?

3. Say: We're going to look closer at the kind of "spiritual fruit" we should bear as we do God's will. Look up Galatians 5:22–23 and have one of your children read the passage aloud. Ask: What kind of fruit does Paul say will be visible in a Christian's life?

4. Now read Galatians 5:19–21. Say: This passage talks about the "works of the flesh" (our sinful nature), which means the fruit we'll produce if we live our lives only for ourselves. Ask: What acts of the sinful nature are listed in this passage?

5. Say: If you think about it, each of us shows the fruit of the Spirit and the fruit of our sinful nature, depending on whether we're serving and obeying God. Tell your children about recent examples of how you displayed both types of fruit. Then ask: Think back over the past few days. Give an example of a time you displayed the fruit of a sinful nature. Describe a time when you displayed the fruit of the Spirit.

6. Say: Let's look at another example of the fruit we should bear as Christians. Read Matthew 28:18–20. Ask:

- What does Jesus command us to do in this passage?
- What do you think it means to "make disciples"?

7. Close your time in prayer, asking God to work through your lives to bear fruit so that people will see love, joy, peace, patience, kindness, goodness, faithfulness, gentleness, and self-control in your lives. Also pray that God will use you to "make disciples."

where do you go from here?

We hope that you have benefited from this study in the Home-Builders Parenting Series and that your marriage and family will continue to grow as you submit to Jesus Christ and build according to his blueprints. We also hope that you will reach out to strengthen other marriages in your local church and community. Your influence is needed.

A favorite World War II story illustrates this point clearly.

The year was 1940. The French army had just collapsed under Hitler's onslaught. The Dutch had folded, overwhelmed by the Nazi regime. The Belgians had surrendered. And the British army was trapped on the coast of France in the channel port of Dunkirk.

Two hundred twenty thousand of Britain's finest young men seemed doomed to die, turning the English Channel red with their blood. The Fuehrer's troops, only miles away in the hills of France, didn't realize how close to victory they actually were.

Any attempt at rescue seemed futile in the time remaining. A thin British navy—the professionals—told King George VI that they could save 17,000 troops at best. The House of Commons was warned to prepare for "hard and heavy tidings."

Politicians were paralyzed. The king was powerless. And the Allies could only watch as spectators from a distance. Then as the doom of the British army seemed imminent, a strange fleet appeared on the horizon of the English Channel—the wildest assortment of boats perhaps ever assembled in history. Trawlers, tugs, scows, fishing sloops, lifeboats, pleasure craft, smacks and coasters, sailboats, even the London fire-brigade flotilla. Ships manned by civilian volunteers—English fathers joining in the rescue of Britain's exhausted, bleeding sons.

William Manchester writes in his epic novel *The Last Lion* that what happened in 1940 at Dunkirk seems like a miracle. Not only were most of the British soldiers rescued but 118,000 other Allied troops as well.

Today the Christian home is much like those troops at Dunkirk—pressured, trapped, demoralized, and in need of help. The Christian community may be much like England—waiting for professionals to step in and save the family. But the problem is much too large for them to solve alone.

We need an all-out effort by men and women "sailing" to rescue the exhausted and wounded families. We need an outreach effort by common couples with faith in an uncommon God. For too long, married couples within the church have abdicated to those in full-time vocational ministry the privilege and responsibility of influencing others.

We challenge you to invest your lives in others, to join in the rescue. You and other couples around the world can team together to build thousands of marriages and families and, in doing so, continue to strengthen your own.

Be a HomeBuilder

Here are some practical ways you can make a difference in families today:

- Gather a group of four to seven couples and lead them through this HomeBuilders study. Consider challenging others in your church or community to form additional HomeBuilders groups.
- Commit to continue building families and marriages by doing another small-group study in the HomeBuilders Parenting Series or the HomeBuilders Couples Series.
- Consider using the *JESUS* film as an outreach. For more information contact FamilyLife at the number or Web site below.
- Host a dinner party. Invite families from your neighborhood to your home, and as a couple share your faith in Christ.
- If you have attended FamilyLife's Weekend to Remember getaway, consider offering to assist your pastor in counseling engaged couples, using the material you received.

For more information about these ministry opportunities, contact your local church or

FamilyLife
PO Box 7111
Little Rock, AR 72223
1-800-FL-TODAY
FamilyLife.com

our problems, God's answers

Every couple has to deal with problems in marriage—communication problems, money problems, difficulties with sexual intimacy, and more. Learning how to handle these issues is important to cultivating a strong and loving relationship.

The Big Problem

One basic problem is at the heart of every other problem in marriage, and it's too big for any person to deal with on his or her own. The problem is separation from God. If you want to experience life and marriage the way they were designed to be, you need a vital relationship with the God who created you.

But sin separates us from God. Some try to deal with sin by working hard to become better people. They may read books on how to control anger, or they may resolve to stop cheating on their taxes, but in their hearts they know—we all know—that the sin problem runs much deeper than bad habits and will take more than our best behavior to overcome it. In reality, we have rebelled against God. We have ignored him and have decided to run our lives in a way that makes sense to us, thinking that our ideas and plans are better than his.

"For all have sinned and fall short of the glory of God." (Romans 3:23)

What does it mean to "fall short of the glory of God"? It means that none of us has trusted and treasured God the way we should. We have sought to satisfy ourselves with other things and have treated them as more valuable than God. We have gone our own way. According to the Bible, we have to pay a penalty for our sin. We cannot simply do things the way we choose and hope it will be okay with God. Following our own plans leads to our destruction.

"There is a way that seems right to a man, but its end is the way to death." (Proverbs 14:12)

"For the wages of sin is death." (Romans 6:23)

The penalty for sin is that we are separated from God's love. God is holy, and we are sinful. No matter how hard we try, we cannot come up with some plan, like living a good life or even trying to do what the Bible says, and hope that we can avoid the penalty.

God's Solution to Sin

Thankfully, God has a way to solve our dilemma. He became a man through the person of Jesus Christ. Jesus lived a holy life in perfect obedience to God's plan. He also willingly died on a cross to pay our penalty for sin. Then he proved that he is more powerful than sin or death by rising from the dead. He alone has the power to overrule the penalty for our sin.

"Jesus said to him, 'I am the way, and the truth, and the life. No one comes to the Father except through me.'" (John 14:6)

"But God shows his love for us in that while we were still sinners, Christ died for us." (Romans 5:8)

"For the wages of sin is death, but the free gift of God is eternal life in Christ Jesus our Lord." (Romans 6:23)

The death and resurrection of Jesus have fixed our sin problem. He has bridged the gap between God and us. He is calling us to come to him and to give up our flawed plans for running our lives. He wants us to trust God and his plan.

Accepting God's Solution

If you recognize that you are separated from God, he is calling you to confess your sins. All of us have made messes of our lives because we have stubbornly preferred our ideas and plans to his. As a result, we deserve to be cut off from God's love and his care for us. But God has promised that if we will acknowledge that we have rebelled against his plan, he will forgive us and will fix our sin problem.

"But to all who did receive him, who believed in his name, he gave the right to become children of God." (John 1:12)

"For by grace you have been saved through faith. And this is not your own doing; it is the gift of God, not a result of works, so that no one may boast." (Ephesians 2:8–9)

When the Bible talks about receiving Christ, it means we acknowledge that we are sinners and that we can't fix the problem ourselves. It means we turn away from our sin. And it means we trust Christ to forgive our sins and to make us the kind of people he wants us to be. It's not enough to intellectually believe that Christ is the Son of God. We must trust in him and his plan for our lives by faith, as an act of the will.

Are things right between you and God, with him and his plan at the center of your life? Or is life spinning out of control as you seek to make your own way?

If you have been trying to make your own way, you can decide today to change. You can turn to Christ and allow him to transform your life. All you need to do is talk to him and tell him what is stirring in your mind and in your heart. If you've never done this, consider taking the steps listed here:

- Do you agree that you need God? Tell God.
- Have you made a mess of your life by following your own plan? Tell God.
- Do you want God to forgive you? Tell God.
- Do you believe that Jesus' death on the cross and his resurrection from the dead gave him the power to fix your sin problem and to grant you the free gift of eternal life? Tell God.
- Are you ready to acknowledge that God's plan for your life is better than any plan you could come up with? Tell God.
- Do you agree that God has the right to be the Lord and Master of your life? Tell God.

"Seek the LORD while he may be found; call upon him while he is near." (Isaiah 55:6)

Here is a suggested prayer:

Lord Jesus, I need you. Thank you for dying on the cross for my sins. I receive you as my Savior and Lord. Thank you for forgiving my sins and giving me eternal life. Make me the kind of person you want me to be.

The Christian Life

For the person who is a follower of Christ—a Christian—the penalty for sin is paid in full. But the effect of sin continues throughout our lives.

"If we say we have no sin, we deceive ourselves, and the truth is not in us." (1 John 1:8)

"For I do not do the good I want, but the evil I do not want is what I keep on doing." (Romans 7:19)

The effects of sin carry over into our marriages as well. Even Christians struggle to maintain solid, God-honoring marriages. Most couples eventually realize they can't do it on their own. But with God's help, they can succeed. To learn more, read the extended version of this article at FamilyLife.com/HomeBuilders.

leader's notes

What is the leader's job?

Your role is more of a facilitator than a teacher. A teacher usually does most of the talking and instructing whereas a facilitator encourages people to think and to discover what Scripture says. You should help group members feel comfortable and keep things moving forward.

Is there a structure to the sessions?

Yes, each session is composed of the following categories:

Warm-Up (5–10 minutes): The purpose of Warm-Up is to help people unwind from a busy day and get to know one another better. Typically the Warm-Up starts with an exercise that is fun but also introduces the topic of the session.

Blueprints (45–50 minutes): This is the heart of the study when people answer questions related to the topic of study and look to God's Word for understanding. Some of the questions are to be discussed between spouses and others with the whole group.

HomeBuilders Project (60 minutes): This project is the unique application that couples will work on between the group meetings. Each HomeBuilders project contains two sections: (1) On your own—questions for husbands and wives to answer individually and (2) With your spouse—an opportunity for couples to share their answers with each other and to make application in their lives.

In addition to these regular features, occasional activities are labeled "Picture This." These activities provide a more active or visual way to make a particular point. Be mindful that people have different learning styles. While most of what is presented in these sessions is verbal, a visual or physical exercise now and then helps engage more of the senses and appeals to people who learn best by seeing, touching, and doing.

What is the best setting and time schedule for this study?

This study is designed as a small-group, home Bible study. However, it can be adapted for more structured settings like a Sunday school class. Here are some suggestions for using this study in various settings:

In a small group

To create a friendly and comfortable atmosphere, we recommend you do this study in a home setting. In many cases the couple that leads the study also serves as host, but sometimes involving another couple as host is a good idea. Choose the option you believe will work best for your group, taking into account factors such as the number of couples participating and the location.

Each session is designed as a sixty-minute study, but we recommend a ninety-minute block of time to allow for more relaxed conversation and refreshments. Be sure to keep in mind one of the cardinal rules of a small group: good groups start *and* end on time. People's time is valuable, and your group will appreciate your respecting this.

In a Sunday school class

If you want to use the study in a class setting, you need to adapt it in two important ways: (1) You should focus on the content of the Blueprints section of each session. That is the heart of the session. (2) Many Sunday school classes use a teacher format instead of a small-group format. If this study is used in a class setting, the class should adapt to a small-group dynamic. This will involve an interactive, discussion-based format and may also require a class to break into multiple smaller groups.

What is the best size group?

We recommend from four to seven couples (including you and your spouse). If more people are interested than you can accommodate, consider asking someone to lead a second group. If you have a large group, you may find it beneficial to break into smaller subgroups on occasion. This helps you cover the material in a timely fashion and allows for optimum interaction and participation within the group.

What about refreshments?

Many groups choose to serve refreshments, which helps create an environment of fellowship. If you plan to include refreshments, here are a couple of suggestions: (1) For the first session (or two) you should provide the refreshments. Then involve the group by having people sign up to bring them on later dates. (2) Consider starting your group with a short time of informal fellowship and refreshments (15–20 minutes). Then move into the study. If couples are late, they miss only the food and don't disrupt the study. You may also want to have refreshments available again at the end of your meeting to encourage fellowship. But remember to respect the group members' time by ending the session on schedule and allowing anyone who needs to leave to do so gracefully.

What about child care?

Groups handle this differently, depending on their needs. Here are a couple of options you may want to consider:

- Have people be responsible for making their own arrangements.
- As a group, hire someone to provide child care, and have all the children watched in one location.

What about prayer?

An important part of a small group is prayer. However, as the leader, you need to be sensitive to people's comfort level with praying in front of others. Never call on people to pray aloud unless you know they are comfortable doing this. You can take creative approaches, such as modeling prayer, calling for volunteers, and letting people state their prayers in the form of finishing a sentence. A helpful tool in a group is a prayer list. You should lead the prayer time, but allow another couple to create, update, and distribute prayer lists as their ministry to the group.

Find additional help and suggestions for leading your Home-Builders group at FamilyLife.com/HomeBuilders.

about the leader's notes

The sessions in this study can be easily led without a lot of preparation time. However, accompanying Leader's Notes have been provided to assist you when needed. The categories within the Leader's Notes are as follows:

Objectives

The Objectives focus on the issues that will be presented in each session.

Notes and Tips

This section provides general ideas, helps, and suggestions about the session. You may want to create a checklist of things to include in each session.

Blueprints Commentary

This section contains notes that relate to the Blueprints questions. Not all Blueprints questions will have accompanying commentary notes. The number of the commentary note corresponds to the number of the question it relates to. (For example, the Leader's Notes, session 1, number 5 in the Blueprints Commentary section relates back to session 1, Blueprints, question 5.)

session one

purposeful discipline

Objectives

To develop an effective plan for disciplining your children, you must first understand that discipline is a biblically mandated responsibility.

In this session, parents will

- enjoy getting to know one another,
- talk about typical problems parents face in disciplining their children,
- examine the importance of discipline as a tool for shaping the character of their children, and
- reflect on why a parent's relationship with his or her children is the foundation for effective discipline.

Notes and Tips

1. Welcome to the first session of the HomeBuilders study *Establishing Effective Discipline for Your Children*. Although it's anticipated that most of the participants will be couples with children, be aware that you may have single parents, future parents, or even one parent from a marriage participating. Welcome everyone warmly and work to create a supportive and encouraging environment.

You'll find certain features throughout this study that are specifically geared toward couples, such as designated couples questions and the HomeBuilders projects. However, we encourage you as the leader to be flexible and sensitive to your group. For example, if you have a single parent in your group, you might invite that person to join you and your spouse when a couples question is indicated in the study. Or, if there are multiple single parents, you may want to encourage them to join together for these questions. Likewise, for the HomeBuilders project at the end of every session, you may want to encourage singles to complete what they can individually or to work with another single parent on the project.

2. If you have not already done so, you'll want to read the information "About Leading a HomeBuilders Group" and "About the Leader's Notes," starting on page 105.

3. As part of the first session, you may want to review with the group some ground rules (see page ix in the introduction).

4. At this first meeting, collect the names, phone numbers, and e-mail addresses of the group members. You may want to make a list that you can copy and distribute to the entire group.

5. Depending on the size of your group, you may spend longer than fifteen minutes on the Warm-Up section. If this

happens, try to finish the Blueprints section in thirty to forty minutes. It's a good idea to mark the questions in Blueprints that you want to be sure to cover. Encourage couples to look at any questions you don't get to during the session when they do the HomeBuilders project.

6. Throughout the sessions in this course, you'll find some questions that are designed for spouses to answer together. The purpose of these questions for couples is to foster communication and unity between spouses and to give couples an opportunity to deal with personal issues. Although couples are free to share their responses to these questions with the group, be sensitive to the fact that not all couples will want to do so.

7. If there is room for more participants, you may want to remind the group that because this study is just underway, they can still invite another couple to join the group.

8. Before dismissing the group, make a special point to tell couples about the importance of the HomeBuilders project. Encourage them to make a date before the next meeting to complete this session's project. Mention that you'll ask about their experience with the project at the next session.

In addition to the HomeBuilders projects, there are six related Parent-Child Interactions beginning on page 83. These are designed to help give parents an opportunity to communicate with their children. Though we recommend that parents try to complete the interactions between group sessions, we know that this will be a challenge. We encourage couples to place a priority on completing the HomeBuilders projects and then doing the Parent-Child Interactions when they have time, whether between sessions or at a later date.

9. You may want to offer a closing prayer instead of asking others to pray aloud. Many people are uncomfortable praying in front of others, and unless you already know your group well, it may be wise to venture slowly into various methods of prayer. Regardless of how you decide to close, you should serve as a model.

Blueprints Commentary

Here is some additional information about various Blueprints questions. (Note: The numbers below correspond to the Blueprints questions they relate to.) If you share any of these points, be sure to do so in a manner that does not stifle discussion by making you the authority with the "right" answers. Begin your comments by saying things like, "One thing I notice in this passage is . . ." or "I think another reason for this is . . ."

3. One of the major reasons many parents don't know how to discipline their children effectively is a lack of good role models. Some group members may have had parents who set poor examples—failed to discipline them, disciplined them too harshly, or even abused them. Our upbringing can lead us to make incorrect conclusions

about discipline. There are also many conflicting opinions in our culture about how to discipline children.

5. Many people say that children are born naturally good, or perhaps with a "blank slate," and only learn selfish or sinful behavior as they grow up. But the Bible tells a different story. Jeremiah 17:9 reminds us that every person's heart—including a child's—is deceitful and sick. Proverbs 22:15 says a child's heart is filled with foolishness. And according to Romans 3:23, a child's heart is sinful, which means that he or she is naturally selfish and rebellious against God.

   Because the natural tendency of our hearts is toward selfishness and foolishness, we must remember that our children must be trained and taught the truth, as well as the consequences of rejecting the truth. They won't seek it on their own.

7. God disciplines us because of his love for us, and his discipline proves that we are indeed his children. If God didn't discipline us, then we would know that he didn't claim us or love us. God's discipline isn't pleasant; it's often painful. But God does it for our own good—not just as a way to correct or reprove disobedience, but also as a blessing that in some way enables us to share in his holiness.

   This should be a model for how we discipline our own children. If we want to reflect God as we discipline them, then we need to do so out of love, and to show

how much we care about them. We should also discipline with a proper goal in mind—not to keep our children in line with our own desires, but to help them grow closer to God.

8. God disciplines us for the same reason we discipline our children—to show us the foolishness of our choices and to draw us back into a closer relationship with him. In some cases God allows us to experience the natural consequences of foolish choices. For example, if you're a salesperson and you treat customers harshly or unfairly, eventually you'll experience the consequences of lower sales or customer complaints, or perhaps you won't receive the promotion you want.

   God may also use other people to discipline us for wrong choices, such as family members, other Christians, supervisors, pastors, and police officers, to name a few. And in God's sovereignty, he may use unexpected events or trials to discipline us.

9. God's love makes it possible and reasonable for us to accept his discipline. We know we can trust God because he loves us completely. Rules and discipline without a loving relationship can easily produce rebellion in a child. The relationship we establish with our children is the foundation for all we do as parents and makes it possible for them to accept our discipline when it comes.

session two

response-abilities

Objectives

Scriptural truths provide the foundation for building character in your children.

In this session, parents will

- consider their responsibility to teach and train their children,
- examine and evaluate their children's "response-ability"— how they respond to authority, to others, and to life's circumstances, and
- discuss the need to be in agreement as they teach and train their children.

Notes and Tips

1. This is the first of four sessions in which couples learn the basics of setting up an overall plan for discipline. Because of diverse backgrounds and experience, it's common for a husband and wife to hold different attitudes about discipline—and they often don't recognize these differences until they begin parenting. These sessions and the related HomeBuilders projects will help couples work together to develop a unified discipline plan.

2. Because this is the second session, group members have probably warmed up to one another but still may not feel free to be completely open about their relationships. Don't force the issue. Continue to encourage couples to attend and to complete the projects.

3. If new people come to this session, during Warm-Up ask them to share the names and ages of their children and why they decided to join the group.

4. If refreshments are planned for this session, make sure arrangements for them have been made.

5. For a more active Warm-Up, you may want to use the "Picture This" exercise. If you choose to do this, you'll need to plan ahead by having something for your group to build or put together. (If you have a large group, provide multiple items that can be assembled in smaller subgroups.) The goal is for the group to struggle with trying to build or create something without the benefit of instructions.

   Here are some ideas for things you could have the group try to build: (1) a puzzle (without seeing the picture); (2) a plastic model (the more pieces, the better!); (3) a building-block creation—for example, if your children have building blocks that include pictures and step-by-step instructions for building various things, bring out the blocks and let the group see only the picture of what they are to build; (4) origami (paper folding)—give everyone a piece of paper and then describe or show a sample of a paper-folding creation they can try to duplicate; and (5) knot tying—if you or someone you know is good at tying elaborate knots, give everyone a strand of twine, show them a complicated knot, and then challenge them to tie the same knot.

6. If you told the group during the first session that you'd be asking them to share something they learned from the first HomeBuilders project, be sure to do so.

7. Question 6 in Blueprints calls for couples to look up different Scripture passages. This approach allows people to simultaneously examine multiple passages. This saves time and gives group members the chance to learn from one another.

8. You may want to ask for a volunteer or two to close the session in prayer. Check ahead of time with a couple of people you think might be comfortable praying aloud.

Blueprints Commentary

2. We're to teach our children the Word of God, as well as to love God and serve him with all their heart and soul. We should weave this instruction throughout the regular aspects of our daily lives.

3. This child receives little guidance and has few bound-aries. It's possible that he or she may even seek out another authority figure to replace the parents.

   It's good to develop a friendship with your child, but as a parent, you are more than a friend—you are God's agent for maturing, encouraging, and protecting your child. Being a parent doesn't prohibit you from also being a friend to a son or daughter, but being a friend cannot preclude your parental responsibilities before God.

6. Here are some of the ways we should relate to others, according to these verses (not an exhaustive list): being affectionate and sympathetic, showing humility, show-ing concern for others, demonstrating love and broth-erly affection, honoring, showing hospitality, living in harmony, and being at peace.

session three

boundaries

Objectives

Setting boundaries is an important element of character building for your children.

In this session, parents will

- affirm the need for boundaries in the lives of their children,
- study God's example of how he sets boundaries for us, and
- analyze some practical examples of setting boundaries.

Notes and Tips

1. Remember the importance of starting and ending on time.

2. As a role model for the group, you should complete the HomeBuilders project. Make a point to encourage couples to do the same.

3. With the completion of this session, you'll be halfway through this study. It's time for a checkup: How's the group going? What has worked well so far? What things

might you consider changing as you approach the remaining sessions?

4. You and your spouse may want to write notes of thanks and encouragement to the couples in your group this week. Thank them for their commitment and contribution, and let them know you're praying for them. (Make a point to pray for them as you write your notes.)

Blueprints Commentary

3. When discussing boundaries, two things are important to remember: (1) Our human nature wants to be free of boundaries—to do whatever it wants—which is why boundaries are so necessary; and (2) it isn't good for a culture, a city, a family, or an individual to operate free of boundaries. If each person were totally free of boundaries, there would be no law, no order, and no morality.

Items that could be added to the list of why boundaries are good (if these aren't raised by the group) include: boundaries provide protection; they provide a sense of security; they teach children there are limits to behavior; they teach the difference between right and wrong; they prepare children to respond to other authorities, including God; and they teach self-discipline.

4. To obey and to fear God (that is, to hold him in reverence and awe) is to prosper and live, to be righteous (Deuteronomy 6:24–25).

6. A challenge to us as parents is to try to make the Bible the primary source for the boundaries we teach our children. For example, are we regularly asking ourselves what guidance the Bible gives in one area or another?

   To help get the ball rolling for this question, you may want to ask the group for examples of boundaries they have for some common areas, such as bedtime, dating, and media (TV, movies, Internet, video games).

8. Too few boundaries can lead to a lack of self-control, less respect for authorities outside the home, and a greater desire to get one's own way. Too many boundaries can lead to rebellion, discouragement, and a lack of self-confidence.

session four

Consequences, Part 1

Objectives

Your children need to experience the consequences of both their good and poor choices.

In this session, parents will

- study how God sets consequences for obedience and disobedience,
- explore the need to establish consequences—both positive and negative—for the choices their children make, and
- discuss specific consequences they can use in training their children.

Notes and Tips

1. This session begins a two-part discussion about setting consequences for children. This can be an emotional subject, especially when corporal punishment (the main topic in the next session) is discussed. Our desire is to meet this subject head-on and challenge people to consider the Bible's teachings. Be prepared for potential disagreements.

2. Some authors and teachers believe that "punishment" should not be part of the discipline process, saying, "We should discipline our children, not punish them," or "God's discipline is positive, but punishment is negative." We have attempted to avoid semantic arguments like this. As we see it, God both punishes and blesses people. And the consequences of each are positive in the sense that they are part of the plan of a God who loves us with an everlasting love.

3. In this session and the next, it's critical for people to realize that reproof and punishment only work in the context of a loving relationship between a parent and child. When people speak of their negative discipline experiences from childhood, the vast majority of problems began with a parent who was distant, unloving, uncaring, and selfish. As discussed earlier, a loving relationship with your child lays the foundation for him or her to accept your discipline when it's necessary.

4. By this time, group members should be getting more comfortable with one another. For prayer at the end of this session, you may want to give anyone an opportunity to pray by asking the group to finish a sentence that starts something like this: *"Lord, I want to thank you for _____."* Be sensitive to those who are not comfortable doing this.

Blueprints Commentary

3. God tells us that we'll be blessed by obeying his Word, and we'll receive curses—punishment or consequences—when we refuse to obey. In the same way, we need to make consequences clear for our children and then follow through with these consequences based on the choices they make.

   It's also important to note that God—through the Bible—clearly explains what behavior is acceptable and unacceptable. If we fail to do the same with our children, we aren't being fair or just with them. It's critical for them to know what is expected of them.

4. Some Christians raise a legitimate concern that rewarding children for right choices appeals too much to their selfish nature and encourages them to obey only because they get something in return. We believe we need to watch for that attitude in our children, but we should also recognize the fact that God does model for us the importance of setting consequences for both bad and good choices. We all have a sin nature, yet God rewards us for obedience.

   When children are praised consistently, it's much easier for them to receive discipline. Praise nurtures a person's spirit with encouragement. Praise is literally pleasing to the ears. It's the flip side of the coin of discipline. If only praise or firm discipline is given, children cannot fully understand how God wants to relate to them.

7. Perhaps the most important conviction we have in this area is to ask God for wisdom regarding what type of discipline is most effective with your children at different ages. We believe that corporal punishment isn't wise or effective with teenagers; we stopped spanking our children sometime between the ages of nine and twelve.

   For this question, depending on the makeup of your group, you may want to have parents divide into subgroups based on the ages of their children. For example, have parents of teens specifically discuss punishments for the thirteen-to-eighteen range and, likewise, the parents of toddlers discuss punishments for two- and three-year-olds. If a couple has children in more than one age category, create subgroups based on the age of the oldest child living at home.

8. Here are a couple of examples for points under this question:

   - A natural consequence for the child whose bicycle was stolen because it wasn't locked up would be for him or her to go without a bike for a specified amount of time.
   - For a child who procrastinated with a school project, instead of bailing out that child by helping with the project, you may be wise to allow your child to get a poor grade so that he or she can experience the consequence of procrastinating.

9. Often we as parents get in the way of what God wants
    to teach our children because we rescue them from the
    consequences of their choices. We've found that one of
    the most difficult things we've had to do in situations
    like these is to sit back and allow a child to struggle with
    the natural results of a poor choice.

session five

Consequences, Part 2
Spanking

Objectives

The Bible isn't silent on the controversial subject of corporal punishment.

In this session, parents will

- contrast differing views about corporal punishment,
- consider what the Bible says about the benefits of spanking, and
- discuss their plan and approach to spanking as a mode of discipline.

Notes and Tips

1. Physical discipline is a controversial subject in our culture today. Since this is the main topic of the session, be prepared for differing opinions. Your goal is to facilitate a positive discussion.

   Encourage an environment where people feel free to discuss the subject without condemning other group members. Challenge people to set aside preconceived notions and take an honest look at what the Bible has to say on this subject.

Blueprints Commentary

2. Corporal punishment has been a normal part of parenting for generations. Though many people grew up with parents who used spanking in an appropriate manner, others did not. Those abuses have led some to conclude that the practice of spanking is abusive and barbaric. This is the attitude frequently reflected in the media. Increasingly we're told that spanking teaches children violence and that other methods of discipline work just as well.

4. If there is any confusion about the word *rod* in Scripture, explain that Bible commentaries generally describe the rod used in Bible times as something like a thin branch from a tree. It was not a weapon.

5. Even before a child is aware of such things as humility or integrity, spanking can be used to begin the learning process regarding consequences and actions. Although a child might not understand repentance, the pain of a spanking that brings tears is almost equivalent to the humility that comes with a repentant spirit. Practiced properly, so that the child isn't injured, and applied consistently with love and affection, spanking literally works itself out of a job. Spanking molds the will. As the will is molded, spanking becomes less necessary. Appeals to God's Word or to the conscience of the child can work well after the will is yielded to the parent.

6. Following are a few examples of the behaviors children may exhibit that reflect the descriptions in Proverbs 6:

- "Haughty eyes"—sassiness, disrespectful words, or a prideful attitude
- "Hands that shed innocent blood"—a child who wants to hurt someone else when he or she is angry or doesn't get his or her way
- "A heart that devises wicked plans"—a child who develops a plan to deceive or manipulate others to accomplish his or her own desires
- "Feet that make haste to run to evil"—a propensity for doing wrong or for making wrong choices
- "A false witness who breathes out lies"—a child who lies about what others do or say
- "One who sows discord among brothers"—a child who leads others to rebel against the authority of parents, or who pits one child against another

session six

Building Your Endurance

Objectives

In running the parenting race, remember that establishing effective discipline is a marathon, not a sprint.

In this session, parents will

- compare parenting to running a distance race,
- identify three keys for persevering in training their children, and
- reflect on their experience with this course.

Notes and Tips

1. As the course comes to an end, this session is a great opportunity for you to try to discern where people may stand with God. Some individuals may never have understood the gospel and don't know what it means to be a Christian. Others may need a better understanding of what it means to walk with Christ on a daily basis. A group experience like this often leads people to examine their spiritual lives and determine how to know God.

   Be prepared to explain the gospel in the group if it seems appropriate. Or be available to meet with group members to discuss this topic further if they would like.

Read through the article "Our Problems, God's Answers" (starting on page 97).

2. Here's a suggestion for making the closing prayer time for this last session special: Have the group form a prayer circle. Then have each person or couple, if they're comfortable doing so, take a turn standing or kneeling in the middle of the circle while the group prays specifically for them.

3. Although this HomeBuilders study has great value, people are likely to return to previous patterns of living unless they commit to a plan for carrying on the progress they've made. During this final session of the course, encourage couples to take specific steps beyond this series to continue to build their homes. For example, you may want to challenge couples who have developed the habit of a "date night" during this study to continue this practice. You may also want to discuss doing another HomeBuilders study.

4. As a part of this last session, devote time to planning for one more meeting—a party to celebrate the completion of this study! (You may want to make this a family party.)

Blueprints Commentary

1. It takes eighteen years just to raise one child to the point of graduating from high school. Especially during the

early years, it's easy to get tired and discouraged from the work it takes day in and day out. To complete the race requires training, perseverance, and a proper attitude.

2. Some parents may choose to reject the truth of God's Word, thinking they know a better way to raise children. Some are entangled with the ghosts of their past and perhaps the fear of making the same mistakes their parents made. Some are too selfish or lazy to discipline their children or to do it consistently. Instead, they let their spouses do it. And some may just feel too tired—they've given up on their responsibilities because they are weary.

4. We believe that an overall goal in parenting is to raise children who will grow up to walk closely with God. As part of this, we emphasize the need to build God-honoring character—to train children to respond rightly to authority, to others, and to life's circumstances. Ultimately we're training our children to respond to God. More important than discipline itself is for parent and child to each have a personal relationship with Christ.

5. Your parental discipline prepares your children to respond properly to discipline and correction from others in authority over them. Ultimately, it prepares them to respond to God's Holy Spirit when the conviction of sin comes and when confession and repentance are necessary. If you don't discipline your children, they may be unresponsive to the Spirit of God.

6. In Christ we find encouragement, strength, and a worthy example when we think we have reached our limit or that a child has done something unforgivable. Whatever we face, Christ has the answer in his life and Word.

Appendix

disciplining your children as they grow

It's impossible to dispense one-size-fits-all advice on discipline, boundaries, and character. However, in the spirit of sharing some practical advice for some of the issues that you and your spouse will face, we offer the following general observations about children during several different phases and a few guidelines to consider. Some children will manifest a number of the issues we list, while others will create unique issues of their own!

This information isn't intended to be exhaustive or academic. It is, however, some of the best advice we've compiled and taught others through our conferences, books, and radio programs. It is offered here in a spirit of encouragement, in our hope that along the way you'll realize your children aren't that different from others and that you can take some practical steps to help them grow! Each section has a listing of certain characteristics to watch for as your child goes through each developmental phase, followed by some recommended boundaries and discipline advice.

> Throughout this feature you'll find alternating "he" and "she" references. Our intent is for the observations to be understood in the generic sense—with all the points applying to both boys and girls.

Birth to Eighteen Months

What to Watch For

1. The first few months of life—when a child is totally dependent on his parents to care for his needs—are absolutely crucial in determining how a child views his world. You may think you are little more than a slave to his needs, but something much more important is going on: By providing food and comfort, you're helping him develop trust in you. If he doesn't develop this trust early on, you'll find it difficult to develop his character and maintain discipline as he grows up.

2. This is also a crucial time for parents to establish control. Your child must be trained to obey and trust you, and she must learn that she won't always get what she wants. Keeping her to a regular schedule produces security and stability—she'll learn to trust that you know what's best.

3. In later infancy, a child begins to discover the ability to act willfully upon his environment. He begins to test limits, and you'll begin to observe willful disobedience. These behaviors may include such things as throwing food and touching things that are off limits.

4. This is the time to establish your relationship. An infant desires touch, nurturing, and verbal tones of affirmation. She wants to bond emotionally with others, and she senses her parents' unconditional acceptance. The emotional environment you set in your relationship will

be critical in developing her emotional security and her
ability to trust you.

Boundaries and Discipline

1. Birth to four months: Work toward creating a regular
   schedule for feeding and sleeping. Be flexible but have a
   standard.
2. Four to eight months: If you're nursing when your baby
   is teething, let him know he cannot bite. Say "No!"
   sternly and swat the child lightly on the thigh. Don't do
   it in anger, but in love let your child know this behavior
   is not acceptable.
3. Six to twelve months: If a child won't stay still while
   you're diapering her, first set her up and let her know
   this behavior is not acceptable. If she doesn't obey,
   lightly swat her quickly once on the leg. Allow your child
   to explore her world as she learns to crawl, pull herself
   to her feet, and then walk. But she must begin to learn
   what she shouldn't touch (oven, electrical outlets, stereo,
   television, and so on). Warn her clearly after the first
   infraction. If she disobeys, swat her lightly on the thigh.
4. Putting a child to bed: As long as a child's needs are met
   and he isn't in any physical danger from her bedrail or
   blanket, it won't cause psychological damage if you let
   him cry. When you put him to bed, let him know you
   won't return until wake-up time. If he cries, let him.
   Eventually he'll cry himself to sleep.

5. When a child throws or plays with food: Begin with a verbal reprimand. If she does it again, remove the food and don't give it back.

Eighteen to Thirty-Six Months

What to Watch For

1. During this stage a child gains increasing control over her muscles and will begin to explore her environment more. She'll begin talking more, and she'll show a greater curiosity about her world. She'll begin to verbalize her needs to her parents, and they won't have to guess as much! This is also an important stage for developing self-confidence and for learning boundaries as she grows in independence. Though she will fight against some of these boundaries, in reality she'll thrive within the rules and routines you establish. They'll give her a needed sense of security.

2. During the first three to five years of life, a child relates almost totally on an emotional level. Reasoning skills are just beginning to be developed. How he feels determines a great deal of his behavior. You'll also notice that he seems like a sponge that soaks up the emotional states of the significant persons in his life. He will often "feel" what you feel.

3. At this age, continue to establish that you are in control and your child is not. If you haven't already started, begin spiritual training. Together, read scriptures, pray,

sing spiritual songs, and read stories. As she begins to talk, recite scriptures and encourage her to join you.

4. A child can establish total control over the household if you allow him. As he grows, he becomes very aware of the consequences of his behavior. If you continually give in to his desires, he learns, "When I want something, I get it." You'll also notice more willful disobedience. When he doesn't get his way, he may use strategies such as whining, yelling, crying, throwing tantrums, and dropping limp to the floor.

5. Increasingly your child will seek to please you. If you're overcontrolling or your expectations are too high, you can cause her to experience frustration and doubt.

6. A critical period—and a big test for you—will be toilet training. Many parents make the mistake of pushing their children to learn this skill too early, which can lead children to experience failure and increase tension between parents and their children.

Boundaries and Discipline

1. As your child interacts with siblings and friends, he'll need your guidance. Children learn how to express and assert themselves with other children during this stage, and you'll need to begin to teach him about respect for others by showing him how to share and how to act unselfishly. He needs to learn not to hit or bite other children and not to take things that belong to someone else.

2. Some of the boundaries you establish will be for your child's protection—things like staying off the street and keeping her hands off knives and tools. If she defies you in these areas, immediate punishment is critical. She won't understand that a car can kill her, but she will understand that running into the street will lead to a spanking.

3. Establishing boundaries can become a huge battle of wills. Remember that you are the adult and that a crucial foundation of your child's character training is learning to submit to your authority.

4. If your child throws a tantrum, our best advice is to not give in to her but let the tantrum run its course until she tires.

5. Careful and consistent enforcement of boundaries is essential. The toddler has gained fantastic motor skills and yet has very little understanding of the world around him. This is the stage in which rebellion can be effectively checked and the child can begin to learn to delay immediate gratification.

6. Decide on different types of discipline for different offenses. Save spanking for those offenses you consider most important in character development.

7. The older your child grows, the more she'll understand when she is disobeying a rule and when she is defying you. When you spank, make sure she understands why.

8. Explain what a "no-no" is, and let your child know the consequences. Make eye contact and ask if he understands. (Children often avoid eye contact in these situ-

ations because they want to avoid responsibility and accountability for what they're hearing.)

9. When in public: Plan ahead and decide what you'll do if your child throws a tantrum. Our suggestion is to take her home and administer discipline there. Let her anticipate the punishment, and let her know ahead of time what you'll do if she misbehaves.

10. Become a student of your child to discern how he responds to different types of rewards and punishments. Some children will require more spankings, and some children only need a mild rebuke for most offenses. Different children respond in different ways, so make your plans accordingly.

Three to Five Years

What to Watch For

1. The preschool years are magical for a child. His abilities to create and imagine begin to blossom and are delightful to observe. Also emerging is your child's identity—sexual and social—which is formed through experimentation with rules for behavior. These years can be magical for parents as well. Now you're able to really talk with your child and take him places. It's important to take advantage of this time while you have it.

2. Continue to watch for all the character issues mentioned for the earlier ages—such as selfishness, defiance, and

willful disobedience. By this age your child will spend much of her time interacting with others, so continue teaching her how to act lovingly and unselfishly.

3. Children often begin telling lies around age three, and stealing seems to begin at age four or five. Realize that your child's inherent selfishness lies at the heart of this behavior. He steals to get what he wants by illegitimate means. He lies to manipulate others to do what he wants or to prevent you from knowing about his bad behavior (and therefore avoid punishment).

4. As in other stages, the most important way to build emotional security in your child is to demonstrate love and unconditional acceptance. She will soak up all the attention you can give her. You need to love her for who she is, not for who you hope or wish she would be.

5. At this stage your child is very receptive to spiritual training. He will believe what you say. If something is important to you, it will be important to him. Use bedtime for stories, prayers, and singing. Read and memorize Scripture together. Encourage him to pray for others. Begin to tell him what God is doing in your life. This is also a good stage to begin family devotions, but remember that children have a short attention span!

6. If you often find yourself yelling at your child in an attempt to make her comply with rules, chances are that you aren't enforcing the boundaries soon enough. Enforce boundaries by taking action rather than by raising the decibel level of your voice.

Boundaries and Discipline

1. Children this age are continuing to develop reasoning skills. They need to know why something is right and why something is wrong. But discussions about why certain behaviors are right or wrong will usually not prove to be fruitful at this age; they need to accept your word. They need to experience immediate consequences for their behavior. That's why spanking remains an effective form of discipline at this age. Other useful alternatives include time-outs, removal of privileges, and allowing natural consequences to occur after certain choices.

2. It's common for a child to make a show of repentance and beg you not to spank. Don't give in—your child still needs to experience the consequences, and then you can see afterward if she truly is sorry for what she has done and will change her behavior.

3. Periodically discuss the different types of discipline you'll administer for different offenses. Make sure your child knows what is expected of him.

4. Spanking for lying: Ask God to give you discernment about when a child is lying—and also which child is lying in a conflict between two siblings. We suggest giving grace for the first lie, but spank for every lie after that. Explain why you are spanking. Also, it's important for a child to admit an obvious lie. If she doesn't, subsequent discipline may be necessary. Pray and ask God to reveal every lie.

5. During this period it's critical to remember that you want to use discipline to bend your child's will without wounding his spirit. A child's spirit is wounded, for example, when you discipline in anger or with a lack of love. A child's spirit is also wounded when you're unfair in your treatment of him and his siblings, or when you punish more than you praise. The older a child grows, the more he will recognize whether you're loving and just in your discipline.

6. If you realize you've made a mistake in how you administered discipline (and it will happen sometimes), we have a simple solution: Use six of the most powerful words ever spoken: "I'm sorry. Will you forgive me?"

7. A word about television: This is a crucial stage for you to set some strict standards and limits for how much television you'll allow your child to watch, and for what shows and films you'll allow her to view. Avoid using television as a babysitter or tranquilizer. Too much TV saps a child's creativity and keeps her away from more meaningful activities. Also, only let your child watch shows you approve, and avoid shows that show violence, sex and sensuality, and disrespect for authority.

Six to Twelve Years

What to Watch For

1. These are years of repetition, when you'll teach and train your child over and over in the same areas. Ask God for

the strength to persevere, and remember Galatians 6:9: "Let us not become weary in doing good, for at the proper time we will reap a harvest if we do not give up" (NIV).

2. We call the ages between eight and eleven the "Golden Years," when your child still listens to you and enjoys spending time with you. You can reason with her and talk seriously about challenges she will face in the future. This is especially important during the last couple of years before adolescence; this is a prime time to discuss the difficult choices she will face during those years about alcohol and drugs, sex and dating, and other teen-age issues.

3. Emphasize spiritual training during these years. Teach your child how to read the Bible, how to pray, and involve him in opportunities to serve others. Use Scripture as you build character and talk about the choices he makes about how he responds to authority, to others, and to life's circumstances.

Boundaries and Discipline

1. Spank primarily for willful disobedience during the first couple of years of this time period. Decrease spanking as your child gets older, and switch to other forms of discipline. By the time the child turns ten, you probably shouldn't be spanking her. Use one of the other forms of discipline you've discussed in this course.

Thirteen to Eighteen Years

What to Watch For

1. Young people increasingly want to establish their independence during this stage and will "pull away" from you emotionally. You'll need to work extra hard at your relationship.

2. Take advantage of the times and settings where your teen is willing to talk. If you find that he opens up around bedtime, be flexible and available.

3. A key point where you release your child to greater independence is when she earns her driver's license. Letting go and entrusting her into God's hands can be difficult. It's important to set clear boundaries for when, where, and how she can drive. It's common for teenagers to feel entitled to greatly expanded freedoms and also to become proud and cocky behind the wheel.

4. It's also common for teenagers to go through a period when they don't feel respect for their parents. Your child may try to argue with you, manipulate you, or make you feel stupid. Like most teenage boys who love debating with their mothers, he may often instigate a debate and try to intimidate you with his size. Don't allow him to gain the upper hand in the relationship.

5. Pay close attention to the peers your child spends time with. Know her peers, the families they come from, and if possible, the values each of those families live by. For good or bad, her friends during this stage will have a tremendous influence in her life.

Boundaries and Discipline

1. Simple declarations of boundaries—"As long as you're living in my house, you'll abide by my rules"—won't work as well as your child grows older. He needs to know the reason for the boundaries you set.

2. Place the greatest importance on boundaries that connect to biblical character issues rather than your personal tastes.

3. You can allow some honest disagreement about some of your decisions, but put a limit on debate and manipulation. Your child still needs to show respect, even when she doesn't feel it.

4. If you're a father, don't allow your son to intimidate his mother. If you're a mother, don't allow your daughter to manipulate her father. You may need to have a heart-to-heart discussion with your children to address the issues of intimidation and manipulation.

5. Set clear boundaries in such areas as driving, curfews, permissible entertainment, and dating relationships. Resist pressure from your teenager to relax boundaries when she tells you, "You're stricter than all my friends' parents."

6. Remember that your child will eventually be totally free to make his own choices after he leaves home. You can prepare him for that time by gradually relaxing your boundaries as he grows older and shows more responsibility.

7. One effective punishment at this age is to assign your child some tiring and menial physical labor, like pulling weeds or scraping paint, to name a couple of tasks.

8. Removal of privileges—such as driving and late curfews—is another effective punishment, because it can cause your child to wake up to the seriousness of a problem. But use this tactic wisely. And be careful not to make other families suffer as a result. For example, if preventing a child from competing in a softball tournament causes problems for teammates and other parents, you might consider another punishment.

more tools for leaders

Looking for more ways to help people build their marriages and families?

Thank you for your efforts to help people develop their marriages and families using biblical principles. We recognize the influence that one person—or couple—can have on another, and we'd like to help you multiply your ministry.

FamilyLife is pleased to offer a wide range of resources in various formats. Visit us online at FamilyLife.com, where you will find information about our:

- getaways and events, featuring Weekend to Remember, offered in cities throughout the United States;
- multimedia resources for small groups, churches, and community networking;
- interactive products for parents, couples, small-group leaders, and one-to-one mentors; and
- assortment of blogs, forums, and other online connections.

FamilyLife is a nonprofit, Christian organization focused on the mission of helping every home become a godly home. Believing that family is the foundation of society, FamilyLife works in more than a hundred countries around the world to build healthier marriages and families through marriage getaways and events, small-group curriculum, *FamilyLife Today* radio broadcasts, Hope for Orphans® orphan care ministry, the Internet, and a wide range of marriage and family resources.

about the authors

Dennis Rainey is the president and a co-founder of FamilyLife (a ministry of Campus Crusade for Christ) and a graduate of Dallas Theological Seminary. For more than thirty-five years, he has been speaking and writing on marriage and family issues. Since 1976, he has overseen the development of FamilyLife's numerous outreaches, including the popular Weekend to Remember marriage getaway. He is also the daily host of the nationally syndicated radio program *FamilyLife Today*. Barbara is an artist and author. Her books include *Thanksgiving: A Time to Remember, Barbara and Susan's Guide to the Empty Nest,* and *When Christmas Came.* The Raineys have six children and sixteen grandchildren.